THE TAO OF CHESS

200 principles to transform your game and your life

by Peter Kurzdorfer,

Author of *The Everything® Chess Basics Book*

Adams Media
Avon, Massachusetts

To Caissa, the goddess of chess

Published by
Adams Media, a division of F+W Media, Inc.
57 Littlefield Street, Avon, MA 02322 U.S.A.
www.adamsmedia.com

ISBN 10: 1-59337-068-7
ISBN 13: 978-1-59337-068-8
Printed in the United States of America.

10 9 8 7 6

Library of Congress Cataloging-in-Publication Data

Kurzdorfer, Peter.
The tao of chess / Peter Kurzdorfer.
p.   cm.
ISBN 1-59337-068-7
1. Chess. I. Title.

GV1445.K87 2004
794'.01—dc22

2003028012

Cover illustration © Russell Illig / Superstock.
Board graphics by Peter Kurzdorfer.

This book is available at quantity discounts for bulk purchases.
For information, call 1-800-289-0963.

Contents

Give your pieces and pawns somewhere to go and something to do.

Tactics are the immediate, forcing moves that disturb the balance of a position in any way.

Captures, checks, promotions, and threats to capture, check, or promote demand an immediate response.

A correct sacrifice is no sacrifice at all. Rather, it is an investment, giving up one thing to obtain something of greater value later on.

Long-range ideas that help you achieve the result you want are called strategy.

Defense is harder than attack, because it's more fun to attack and, psychologically, the burden of defense is often hard to bear.

Combinations and plans have a better chance of working when they are backed up with good calculation.

The relationships between pieces and pawns are intricate. Understanding these relationships is essential to good chess play.

You should know which pieces and pawns to exchange and when to exchange them.

Predicting the future is not easy, especially when you have an opponent who wants a different outcome.

Sometimes, the game will start out with a bang. Other times it may start out with a yawn. How much do you know about your opening?

After the pieces have come into the action and the kings are settled in, the middlegame takes over.

The endgame is not necessarily the end of the game, as the name would indicate.

PART II: HUMAN MATTERS

Knowing yourself includes knowing your style, proclivities, will to win, capacity for hard work, and so many other bits of information about yourself.

You don't play chess in a vacuum. Your opponent is trying to thwart everything you do.

Visualizing possible future positions while looking at something else is one of the most important skills to strive for.

It's not necessarily bad to fear your opponent, his moves, or any of his ideas. But you need to face those fears squarely and not give in to them.

Chapter 36: Patience................................... **214**
All strong players possess this virtue in abundance, at least during a closely contested game.

Chapter 37: Luck **218**
If you think luck doesn't play a part in chess, you probably haven't played a whole lot.

Chapter 38: Practice................................... **221**
You will learn to make good decisions by making many decisions.

Chapter 39: Study................................... **226**
Find out what those who have gone before you have learned, and you build up a good foundation of knowledge.

Chapter 40: Passion **230**
If chess has not captured your soul, you probably will not do as well as one who is enthralled by Caissa.

Chapter 41: Knowledge **233**
There have been more books written about chess than about all other games combined. In addition, there are databases with millions of chess games. You can spend your entire life learning about chess, but you will never learn all there is to know about it or come close to examining every important game that has ever been played.

Chapter 42: Excuses **238**
Why do you lose? Finding excuses for not performing at your best is easy to do. But it can also retard possible later improvement by taking your attention away from the real problems.

Acknowledgments

I have been deeply involved with the world of chess for more than thirty years. I have learned from watching, analyzing, playing, kibitzing, reading, teaching, solving, coaching, organizing, writing, editing, directing tournaments, participating in leagues, clubs, camps, classes, tournaments, simultaneous exhibitions, matches, and so many other activities that thinking about it makes my head spin.

In order to acknowledge all the people that helped hone my understanding of chess, not to mention all the people who helped hone my understanding of life, I would have to list practically everybody I have come in contact with, either in person, over the phone, through e-mail, books, magazines, Web sites, other media, and so on. This is simply impossible. I couldn't possibly remember them all to begin with, and would inevitably leave out a great many who have helped my growth in chess and life. Besides, the list of what I would remember would be much too long. Therefore, I want to thank everyone who has contributed to my understanding. This includes all my opponents, students, teachers, coworkers, bosses, colleagues, teammates, contributors, authors I have read, my wonderful, supportive family, and anyone I have come in contact with in any way. Without all of you, I would not be the person I am, and would not have the understanding I have about chess as well as life. Thank you all!

—Peter Kurzdorfer

Introduction

*"Chess is a sea where a gnat may drink
and an elephant may bathe."*
—Old (Asian) Indian proverb

*"Chess, like love, like music, has the power
to make men happy."*
—Siegbert Tarrasch

*"In answering the question 'Which is the greater game, chess
or checkers?,' I must, in all frankness, favor chess."*
—Newell W. Banks (Blindfold checker champion
of the world)

"Chess is as much a mystery as women."
—C.J.S. Purdy

*"Others may talk of the Round Table with its 50 knights,
but I greatly prefer the square table with only four knights."*
—Willard Fiske

Tao is a Chinese concept (originally spelled out by Lao Tzu in the sixth century B.C.), meaning "the way." The way, as advanced by Lao Tzu, advocates simplicity and selflessness. Tao is a method of, or perhaps, a set of guidelines for attempting to reach the truth at a progressively deeper level. This seeking brings us closer to understanding whatever we are dealing with. Through understanding we can achieve peace of mind, knowing that we are doing all we can to get at true meaning. Simplicity is necessary to avoid getting confused with irrelevancies, which are everywhere. Selflessness is necessary in order to get a detached view, uncluttered by ego. So what can a religious philosophy have to do with chess?

Following the principles of good, sound chess play will improve your game and your enjoyment of the game; it will also give you a progressively deeper understanding of the game, just as Tao gives you a progressively deeper understanding of life.

But the Tao of Chess means far more than that. By seeking the underlying truth in whatever position that may be before you, you will develop a habit of searching for the truth, and that may well be something you will practice for the rest of your life. Searching for the truth takes energy and determination. Therefore, it is not something many people normally do. But developing habitual thought processes can change all that. That's the wonderful thing about habits. Once you have them in place, they are hard to break.

I am reminded of Lajos Portisch, a great Hungarian chess grandmaster and teacher during the latter part of the twentieth century, who advocated simplicity and economy in his pupils' play. The same concepts are abundantly apparent in the play of the Cuban world chess champion José Raúl Capablanca (1888–1942). And the play of the great one, Bobby Fischer, the American bad boy and world champion, was always filled with very simple concepts ruthlessly carried out.

For instance, Fischer was playing Black against Anthony Saidy in a 1963 New York City encounter when the following position appeared on the board:

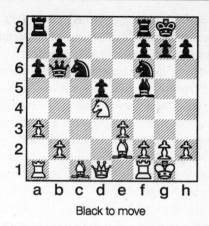

Black to move

Black has a nice lead in development, while nothing else seems to be going on. But this was enough for Fischer, who proceeded to exchange off his well-developed pieces in order to get a superior endgame with a good knight against a bad bishop: 1. ... Nxd4 2. Qxd4 Qxd4 3. exd4 Rac8 4. Bd1 Bc2 5. Be3 Bxd1 6. Rfxd1 Rc2 7. Rd2 Rfc8 8. Rxc2 Rxc2 9. Rc1 Rxc1+ 10. Bxc1 Nd7 11. Kf1 Nf8 12. Ke2 Ne6 13. Kd3.

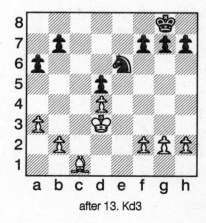

after 13. Kd3

Fischer went on to win the ending. By cutting out a lot of unnecessary complications and getting to the core of the position, Fischer managed to get an easy endgame win.

Any time there is a clear path ahead, travel down it without getting distracted by irrelevancies, and you will reach your goal.

Many of the principles of good chess play seem quite simple on the surface—bring out a new piece with each move, nail down a weakness and only then attack it, passed pawns have a lust to expand—all very obvious when we stop to think about them. This is often the hallmark of a profound truth: something that becomes obvious when stated in simple terms.

Many of the principles in this book may seem contradictory. Chess is fantastically complex. If you come to appreciate the underlying idea behind each principle and the special characteristics of the position before you, these contradictions can be sorted out and understood. One example should illustrate how you can reconcile such internal contradictions:

The Ruy Lopez Exchange Variation begins 1. e4 e5 2. Nf3 Nc6 3. Bb5 a6 4. Bxc6.

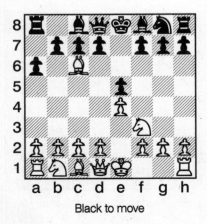

Black to move

Black will capture the bishop in order to restore material balance. But how? One principle states that it is better to capture toward the center with your pawns when there is a choice. Clearly, this indicates 4. ... bxc3 is the correct move. Yet chess theory frowns on this move, considering the alternate capture, 4. ... dxc3 to be much better. How can that be? Is the principle of capturing toward the center with your pawns no good?

Not at all. The principle about capturing toward the center with your pawns is an excellent idea to keep in mind at all times. The center squares are simply more important than other squares most of the time. Therefore, controlling these squares in any way you can, such as capturing toward the center, is usually desirable.

But sometimes another principle may conflict with the principle of capturing toward the center, and you have to decide which is the more appropriate principle. In this case, a glance at the figure reveals Black's major problem in the position: He is behind in development. White has two pieces out and about while Black has none. Of course, Black is about to capture one of those pieces. Still, it will then be White's move, and he is free to develop yet another piece.

Developing a new piece with each move is an underlying idea behind many principles, such as "Don't move the same piece twice in the opening if you can help it," and the endgame principle "The king is a fighting piece; use it." This development principle is simply more important in the figure than capturing toward the center. By recapturing with the d-pawn, Black opens up the d-file for his queen and the c8-h3 diagonal for his bishop. Thus, the capture away from the center helps Black to catch up in development quicker, and that turns out to be more important in this specific situation. In fact, since the d-file is opened to Black's queen, and the squares d4 and d5 are on that file, you can even see how Black is actually controlling more center squares in this case with the away-from-the-center recapture.

By learning to choose between the principles of good chess play in a given situation, you may well improve or learn to enjoy other aspects of life more as well. Chess is, after all, a competition with strict rules, like many sports and games; also like in business, finance, or law. And who doesn't want to know the profound truths at the bottom of that which directly affects him?

This book is divided into two sections, encompassing technical matters and human matters. Together, the 200 principles in this book lead the way to the deeper truths of chess.

Part I
Technical Matters

Chess involves a lot of technical material. A player has to be able to define en passant and know how a bishop moves, what checkmate looks like, and what an Exchange is worth, for instance. These technical details should be second nature for anyone interested in getting the most out of the game.

The most difficult part for humans is, strangely enough, the easiest part for computers: Looking into the future. What does the position after a series of moves look like in comparison to the position you see before you? Accurately visualizing the positions and then assessing their relative merits while looking at another position is a difficult, though not impossible, exercise. There are principles that will help you here, but they involve doing hard work. Then again, if chess were easy, nobody would bother to spend time with it, play it, or read or write books about it.

Chapter 1

The Board

How well do you know the playing field? The chessboard is a big square consisting of sixty-four smaller squares lined up in rows of eight-by-eight. Thirty-two, or half of these squares, are light, and another thirty-two are dark. The lines made up of eight squares in a row along the vertical direction of the board are called files—these are lettered. Those along the horizontal direction of the board are called ranks—these are numbered. The diagonal lines (made up of varying numbers of squares touching at the corners) are all made up of squares of one color.

Principle 1: If you control more than half of the squares on the board, you have an advantage.
The first principle is quite obvious, once you realize that controlling squares means that any enemy piece or pawn that trespasses on those squares is vulnerable to capture.

But there's more to dominating the board than possessing an advantage in space. Controlling more squares is fine, surely, but how many more squares, and what exactly do we mean by controlling? Is it enough to have a bishop oversee a square, or do we need a pawn? Does occupying a square with a piece or pawn constitute control?

The answers to all these questions depend on the position at hand. If they were that easy to answer in general, there would be no need for the literally millions of chess books on the market, or for the hundreds, perhaps even thousands of games played every day.

Your control must also be enduring to give you an advantage. For instance, after 1. e4 Nf6 2. e5 Nd5 3. d4 (Alekhine's Defense), White controls the center—for now. But after Black plays moves such as ... d7-d6 and ... Nb8-c6 and perhaps ... g7-g6 and ... Bf8-g7, White's center will come under a powerful attack, and it won't be so clear who controls the center after all.

It's inescapable. If you want to know whether you really control more squares than your opponent, you have to look into the future a bit. You simply cannot separate the element of time in chess from other elements, such as the control of squares.

♟ ♞ ♜ ♛

A politician running for office needs to control more than half the votes in order to be elected. This flows from the same principle. Wolves and other wild animals probably understand this principle better than most humans (other than politicians) do. They know about the importance of territory, which is their version of squares.

Principle 2: A knight on the rim is grim.

This is a profound bit of advice I probably first came across in the writings of Fred Reinfeld. It is a very specific statement that is meant to incorporate much more than it actually says.

Perhaps a better way to state this principle is pieces that have few squares in their sight are not very useful. This applies not only to knights on the edge of the board, but also to bishops encumbered by their own pawns and rooks stuck in the corner without any open or even half-open files available.

This is really a mobility principle. Knights are usually poor on the side of the board because they don't have many places to go from there. By understanding this underlying truth, you will be able to spot instances where this specific guideline isn't operative and another principle may carry more weight. The following figure shows the truth of this principle:

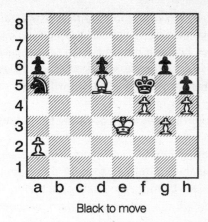

Black to move

Although it is Black's move, there's really nothing she can do to thwart White's plans. White's king can hang around the kingside, forcing the Black monarch to give way, and dine on Black pawns. Or he can head to the queenside to gobble the immobile knight and pawn, followed in both cases by marching and promoting a White pawn. The main reason all this is possible is that Black is really playing down a piece. Her knight on the rim is completely useless.

♟ ♞ ♜ ♛

Don't get into a situation where you don't have options. Putting all your eggs in one basket backfires when the basket breaks.

Principle 3: Place your pawns on the opposite color square as your bishop.

This principle is another way of saying that pieces and pawns should complement each other. Since bishops and pawns each capture diagonally, placing the bishop and pawn on opposite color squares simply gives you more places where you can make captures.

Putting bishops and knights on the same color squares is another way to follow this principle, as is fighting with a queen and knight versus a queen and bishop. Strive to get the most out of your pieces at all times.

This principle embodies the essence of teamwork. There are many ways in which you can avoid duplication of effort. In an office team, each employee does her own job. In a sports team, each player has his own assignment. In a barbershop quartet, each voice sings its own part. Otherwise, the project, game, or song will break down.

Principle 4: The path from a1 to a8 is the same length as the path from a1 to h8.
This one seems anti-intuitive. The diagonal path looks longer, therefore it must be longer. But on the chessboard this simply isn't true. It takes a king at least seven moves to cover either path.

However, although the diagonal path is not longer, taking such a path can often give your piece more options. For instance, there are various ways to get from a1 to a8 in seven moves. One of them is a1-a2-a3-a4-a5-a6-a7-a8. Another is a1-b2-c3-d4-d5-c6-b7-a8.

If you think that it doesn't make any difference, take a look at the following famous study by the Czech grandmaster Richard Reti.

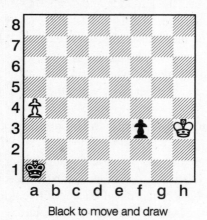

Black to move and draw

Black's task looks impossible at first glance. But it comes in two parts, and that is the key. One task is to catch the a-pawn. This task is impossible by itself. The other task is to promote the f-pawn safely. This is also an impossible task by itself. But by combining the tasks by taking a diagonal route, Black succeeds in either one or the other:

1. ... Kb2 2. a5 Kc3 3. a6 Kd3 and the White pawn is going to promote safely, but so is the Black pawn. If Black tries to stop that earlier, we get 3. Kg3 Kd4 4. a6 Ke3 and again both pawns promote. If Black stops that with 4. Kxf3 then after 4. ... Kc6 the a-pawn also dies.

♟ ♞ ♜ ♛

It's not so much where you are going as it is how you will get there. The various routes have to be carefully chosen, and those who pay attention to what goes into each alternative route will get the most out of whatever trip they are taking.

Chapter 2

The Pieces

"The pawn is the soul of chess."
—Attributed to Philidor

Know the tools you are given to work with; they're all you have. The pieces and pawns (pawns are not considered pieces) come in six types, and each of them has peculiarities that you should be aware of.

Principle 5: Leave the pawns alone, except for center pawns and passed pawns.
This principle stems from the inherent weakness in all pawns: They cannot move backward. Once a pawn has moved, the squares it can no longer control are gone from its sights forever, or until it promotes to something else, in which case it is no longer a pawn. Thus you cross the Rubicon with each pawn move.

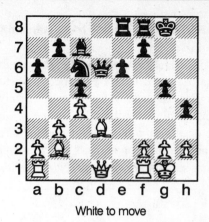

White to move

This is a rather graphic example of what happens when you don't leave the pawns alone. Although Black threatens mate next move, she loses quickly because she has moved the g-pawn out, creating a gash in the defense that cannot be repaired. White swoops in easily with 1. Bh7+ Kxh7 2. Qh5+ Kg8 3. Qh8 mate.

Center pawns and passed pawns (pawns facing no enemy pawns on the file they are on or on either adjacent file) are exceptions to this principle for different reasons. Center pawns are good to move because they then occupy central squares, and they also open up lines for bishops and queens to enter into the contest. Thus the new weaknesses can be tolerated because of all the good that comes out of such moves. Passed pawns want to move simply because they are on the path to promotion. So, although they leave weak squares in their path, the end result is generally well worth the weaknesses.

♟ ♞ ♜ ♛

Making a commitment takes a certain amount of thought and preparation. You don't want to make too many serious commitments without taking the time to weigh how they will affect your game. That's exactly what you do when you make too many pawn moves.

Principle 6: **In order to get the most from your knights, give them strong support points.**

The knight is the only unit that doesn't have the capability of moving to an adjacent square. It is by nature a jumper. Therefore, the knight's position can be as clogged up as you like, and the knight won't suffer in terms of potential mobility at all.

But this piece does best with a well-supported base of operations. So place him in a hole (in your opponent's area of the board if possible) and make sure he has support. Pawn support is especially helpful.

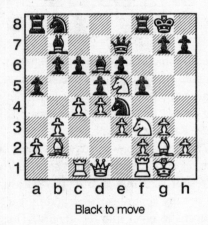

Black to move

White's knight on e5 is ideally placed, while Black's knight on e4, though well placed, is not in as good a position, since White could play the pawn move f2-f3 at some point in the future.

♟ ♞ ♜ ♛

No man is an island. Support from family, friends, or colleagues is essential in getting anything of value accomplished. In that way we are all knights: We are at our best with lots of support.

Principle 7: **To be at their best, bishops require open diagonals and attackable weaknesses.**

The chessboard prelates move on diagonals only, so anything friendly blocking the way reduces their power. A bishop placed on the same color squares as his own pawns is referred to as a bad bishop. Such a piece has no mobility—nowhere to go, nobody to see. A blocked bishop is often referred to as a tall pawn, but he often has even less power than a pawn, since he can't move forward one square like a pawn can.

On the other hand, a good bishop is one without friendly pawns on the same colored squares. The friendly pawns are on opposite colored squares, so that the pawns and the bishop complement each other.

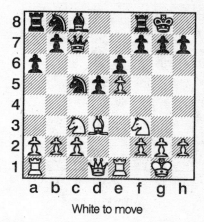

White to move

In the diagram, White's bishop is good, while Black's bishop is bad. The difference is immediately apparent in White's combination, the classical bishop sacrifice, which begins with 1. Bxh7+ Kxh7 2. Ng5+. The Black king is exposed to the remaining White pieces, while the Black queenside pieces sleep. Of what use was the c8-bishop through all this? Let your bishops breathe the free air of uncluttered diagonals.

♟ ♞ ♜ ♛

Cooperative action is efficient action. Lack of action due to a lack of opportunity is very inefficient indeed.

Principle 8: Rooks require open files and ranks in order to reach their full potential.

This principle is very similar to the last one. The rook is very much like the bishop in that he operates best on open and half-open lines. The difference is that the rook uses ranks and files rather than diagonals.

A rook is potentially stronger than any bishop is because he can attack every square on the board quickly, while the bishop can only attack half of the squares. But the rook's power is only an untapped potential until he is given open lines on which to do damage.

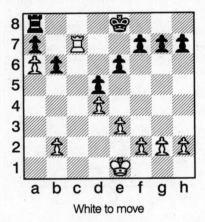

White to move

Compare how rooks are used in this example. The White rook keeps the Black rook and king tied to the defense of weak pawns, thus giving the White king time to come over to the queenside to mop up. Meanwhile, the Black rook takes on the menial job of defending the a-pawn. If she leaves her task, the White rook will swoop in, capturing the pawn, and the White a-pawn will soon promote.

Successful people go after what they want, and in that they resemble successful rooks. Unsuccessful people don't go after what they want nor do they freely interact with others. In that way, they resemble unsuccessful rooks.

Principle 9: Don't bring the queen out too early.

This may seem a paradoxical principle at first glance, but it turns out the queen's great power is actually a handicap early in the game. Any lesser unit will threaten her with impunity, thus forcing her to move again and again, while the enemy brings new pieces into the fray.

A case in point is a naive attempt called the Scholar's Mate. After 1. e4 e5 2. Bc4 Nc6 White plays 3. Qh5, hoping Black will miss the threat of mate. But after Black defends with 3. ... Qe7 4. Nc3, we get 4. ... Nf6, and the White queen has to back up, while Black now has a chance to get her pieces into the game faster.

But notice that Black also moved her queen early. The difference is that she is not as vulnerable on e7 as White's queen was on h5.

Following this principle is tricky. What constitutes "too early"? The Center Game (1. e4 e5 2. d4 exd4 3. Qxd4 Nc6 4. Qe3) and the Scandinavian Defense (1. e4 d5 2. exd5 Qxd5 3. Nc3 Qa5) are both considered respectable openings, despite the early queen development. What are we to make of the Ruy Lopez Exchange Variation (1. e4 e5 2. Nf3 Nc6 3. Bb5 a6 4. Bxc6 dxc6), where 5. Nxe5 is considered inferior because of either 5. ... Qd4 or 5. ... Qg5, in either case recovering the pawn while gaining a positional advantage by the early queen move?

It sometimes requires deep thought in order to understand whether the queen is entering the game too early. The answer has to be found in the potential variations, in which you determine whether the early queen move accomplishes its objectives. It is not an easy principle to master.

The underlying truth to this principle is that valuable units should not be exposed before the way has been sufficiently prepared: The general should not lead his army into battle on the front lines; the celebrity or statesman does not make the initial contact.

But it's important not to hold back your strongest forces for too long. It's a delicate task to determine just when too early is, and there are no easy answers to fall back on. Every instance requires examination on a case-by-case basis.

Chapter 3

Development

Wake the pieces up from their initial slumber or pay the consequences. Chess is a team sport, with the pieces making up the teams and the players' super coaches who attempt to get the most out of their piece[s]. One way to do that is to pour more players into the action than the opponent. It makes little sense to attempt two-on-five breaks.

Principle 10: Connect your rooks as soon as you can.
When your rooks defend each other, that means all of your other pieces have been cleared out of their starting positions. This is something you strive for as quickly as you can if there are lots of open lines. Your pieces need to be out and about in such situations, both in order to generate an attack on your opponent and to be ready to defend any attack thrown at your army.

Rooks also need open lines in order to be effective, and usually that can best be accomplished by opening up central files. Of course the rooks can get to those files most efficiently by traveling along the home rank, and they can do that best if they are not blocked by friendly pieces.

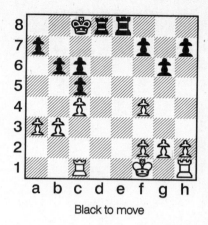

Black to move

Black's rooks are connected and ready for action. White's are sep-
arated, since his king is in the way. Which side do you prefer?

♟ ♞ ♜ ♛

Communication is the key word here. When each member of your
team knows what is going on, a lot can be accomplished. When there
are obstacles in the way and communications break down, major
trouble is imminent.

Principle 11: **Develop a new piece with each move in the opening.**
This guideline is based on common sense. The more pieces you throw
at your opponent, the harder it is for him to resist.

There are almost an infinite number of examples, but one will suffice. In the Scotch Gambit, after 1. e4 e5 2. Nf3 Nc6 3. d4 exd4 4. Bc4
Bc5, the move 5. Ng5?! begins a premature attack.

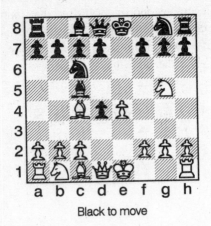

Black to move

After 5. Ng5 White is attacking with his only developed pieces. How can Black refute the attack? Certainly not by making the same mistake: 5. ... Ne5?! gives White a good game after 6. Nxf7 Nxf7 7. Bxf7+ Kxf7 8. Qxh5+ g6 9. Qxc5.

But if Black brings a new piece into play with 5. ... Nh6, White's combination blows up in his face: 6. Nxf7 Nxf7 7. Bxf7+ Kxf7 8. Qxh5+ g6 9. Qxc5 and after 9. ... d6 the White queen has to retreat while more Black pieces pour into the game.

♟ ♞ ♜ ♛

The underlying principle behind developing new pieces with every move is the same as that behind the familiar saying "many hands make light work." Whenever we work or play as part of a team, or whenever we make new friends, we are lightening our own burdens. Sharing the load, in life, as in chess, helps us on our way.

Principle 12: Don't move the same piece twice in the opening if you can help it.

The key phrase here is "if you can help it." Obviously, after 1. e4 e5 2. Nf3 Nc6 3. Bb5 a6 White can't move anything other than his bishop, or he will lose it. The reason for this principle is that any time you move the same piece a second or third time that represents a wasted opportunity for getting a different piece into action.

One example, in which one side doesn't move the same piece again and again, while the other does, is sufficient. After 1. e4 e5 2. Nf3 d6 3. d4 Bg4 4. dxe5 Bxf3 5. Qxf3 dxe5 5. Bc4:

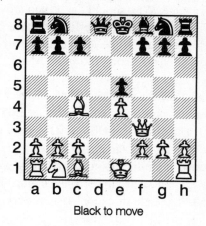

Black to move

We can see that Black has moved a bishop twice and that it is gone. White, on the other hand, has moved three pieces once each. He has a big lead in development and is threatening checkmate. Which side do you prefer?

The truth of this principle is the sound idea of efficiency. Let each team member do the job he is supposed to do, and all the jobs will get done.

Principle 13: Develop knights before bishops.

Though usually presented in this form, this principle is really better stated "Develop your pieces in the most flexible manner." The reason knights are usually developed before bishops is that we usually know where the knights are best placed—at c3 and f3 for White and c6 and f6 for Black. Bishops, on the other hand, have many choices, and it is usually better to wait a bit before committing them to one particular diagonal.

An exception to this principle shows the real reason behind it. The Four Knights' Game begins 1. e4 e5 2. Nf3 Nc6 3. Nc3 Nf6. But the Ruy Lopez (3. Bb5) is generally accepted as a more serious attempt by White to get an advantage. Why should the bishop move be better than the knight move? Because the White light-square bishop is well-placed on the a4-e8 diagonal, White is ready to castle, and the White b1-knight might be better off taking the route b1-d2-f1-e3 or g3 later in the game (Black has weakened the f5-square with 1. ... e5).

This thinking may seem convoluted, but well over a hundred years of experience in master games has shown that 3. Bb5 is in fact more flexible than 3. Nc3. Therefore, it conforms to the spirit of the principle.

♟ ♞ ♜ ♛

Flexibility is once again the dominant factor in a chess principle. Leaving yourself with options is almost always much better than committing yourself to one course of action: If it goes wrong, there is no recourse.

Chapter 4

The Center

"1. e4 is best by test."
—Bobby Fischer

"After the first move 1. e4, White's game is in its last throes."
—Julius Breyer

Inject your game with life by bringing out the best in all your pieces and pawns. Place them in the center or get them to look at the center from afar. The most extreme example is to place a knight on an empty board. Depending on how close to the center or how close to the edge it is, the piece can control as little as two squares or as many as eight squares.

Constantly striving to control the central squares is one of the hallmarks of a good player.

Principle 14: A wing attack is best met by a counterattack in the center.

This principle confuses some players. Why isn't it better to defend on the wing being attacked? Why is no mention made of attacking the king?

The idea behind this principle is that pieces and pawns are at their best in the middle of the board. With that bit of knowledge in mind, why play defensive moves where your pieces are not at their best? This principle applies wherever your king is and wherever your opponent's king is.

Therefore, if you come under attack on the side of the board, repulse that attack with the best weapons you have available, namely, your central pieces.

Take the Two Knights' Defense as an example of this principle in action: 1. e4 e5 2. Nf3 Nc6 3. Bc4 Nf6 4. Ng5.

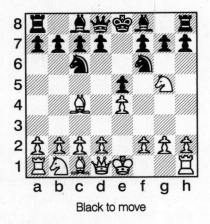

Black to move

Here is a flank attack. How does Black respond? By attacking in the center with the pawn sacrifice 4. ... d5, which also makes room for more Black pieces (the queen and light-square-bishop) to enter the game quickly.

♟ ♞ ♜ ♛

Make the most of what you have, especially when things are tough and you are under the gun. The way to beat off disaster when trouble strikes is to be alert and able to call on whatever resources are available to you.

Principle 15: Before beginning a wing attack, make sure your center is secure.

Wilhelm Steinitz first explained this principle during the late nineteenth century. He was reacting to the many unsound attacks prevalent in his day. A player can attack with impunity only after his center is secure. Therefore, an attack can only be successful against top-notch defense if it is well prepared, Steinitz taught. That means the attacker must guard against the counterattack in the center of Principle 14.

A perfect illustration of this principle in action is the following finale:

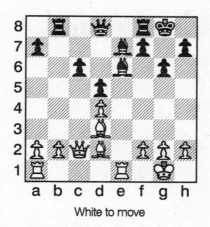

White to move

White has the center well under control. He also has a weakened Black king to attack. The game therefore winds up with 1. Bh6 Re8 2. Rxe6 fxe6 3. Bxg6 hxg6 4. Qxg6+ Kh8 5. Qg7 mate. There was no chance for a counterattack in the center.

Be prepared. Your car should be tuned up, your knives sharp, your teeth in good shape, and your heating system in good repair. Everything you have should be at its best at all times. That way, when the unexpected happens, you are as ready as you can be.

Principle 16: Centralize your pieces to make them powerful.

Place an empty board before you and put a knight on various squares. Compare its powers when it is on the corner, on the rim, or in the middle. Next do the same with a bishop. Do it with a queen, a king, and finally a pawn. Even the king and the pawn are more powerful when they are away from the side of the board. Only the rook is a special case. As long as the ranks and files are open, a rook will have fourteen squares to oversee anywhere you place him.

But the other pieces make a strong case for why masters try to control the center. Any piece that moves diagonally will have more power in the center, and the knight is even more extreme than that!

Take another look at the figure from page 6.

Black to move and draw

You were introduced to this study under Principle 4, which deals with various paths. Now look at the same study and concentrate on the tremendous power the Black king gains from traveling through the center.

A player's power is proportional to her number of choices. When you have more choices to make, you have more potential power. This is one part of the principle that "knowledge is power"; you can't make a choice if you don't know the choices you have. Give all your pieces the power they deserve, just like you give your family, friends, colleagues, and teammates all that they deserve. You will be richly rewarded.

Principle 17: **When choosing between two pawn captures, it's generally better to capture toward the center.**

This principle flows directly from the last principle. Since pieces are more powerful on central squares, the more you can control those squares, the better your game is. Here is an example:

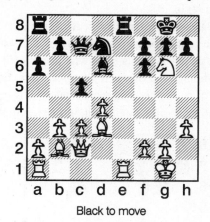

Black to move

Black has just lost a piece on g6 and is therefore compelled to get it right back. But how? The capture 1. ... fxg6 leaves him with one set of doubled pawns, but weakens the square e6, which is right in the middle of the hotly contested e-file. It also leaves the Black king vulnerable along the newly opened c4-g8 diagonal.

The capture toward the center, on the other hand, 1. ... hxg6, keeps e6 under firm control and brings the h-pawn closer to the center. It also keeps the Black king safe from molestation via any stray open diagonals. Black now has two sets of doubled pawns, but notice how they control a lot of potential penetration squares in Black's position: e6, e5, f5, g5, h5, not to mention f6, g6, and h6. That's a lot of defensive power!

Just keep in mind that other principles, such as quick development of forces or king safety, may conflict with this one. Never capture toward the center automatically. Rather, assess the likely impact of each capture each time one becomes possible.

Look to the future when making any choices. You can only predict so much with any degree of accuracy, but you can follow sound principles in making your choices.

Principle 18: Play to control the center, whether Classically or in the hypermodern style.

Since pieces are stronger in the center, it only makes sense that you want to control the center. But how are you going to do this?

The Classical center consists of pawns in the center supported by pieces. Wilhelm Steinitz and Siegbert Tarrasch were the biggest proponents of this style of center control, which was in vogue near the end of the nineteenth century and the beginning of the twentieth century.

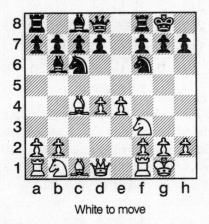

White to move

White has the Classical center and gets a big advantage by going for more and more of the central squares with 1. e5 Ne8 2. d5 Ne7 3. d6.

The hypermodern center was a later development. In the early 1900s, many chess masters questioned the Classical teachings of chess. Among these masters were Richard Reti, Aron Nimzovich, and the world champion-to-be Alexander Alekhine. They—and others—thought a player could control the center from afar with pieces operating from the flank. They used the fianchetto development of the bishop and allowed their opponents to build up a big pawn center only to strike it down later with flank pawn thrusts and piece play.

The hypermoderns devised openings like 1. Nf3 d5 2. c4 (The Reti Opening), 1. e4 Nf6 2. e5 Nd5 (Alekhine's Defense), and 1. d4 Nf6 2. c4 e6 3. Nc3 Bb4 (The Nimzo-Indian Defense).

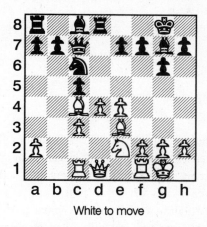

White to move

Black has a hypermodern center. The central area of the board is populated by White pawns, but Black has good play against this center with her fianchettoed bishop on g7, rook on the d-file, c5-pawn and c6-knight, all striking at the d4-strong point in White's game.

However a player does it, control of key squares is the main feature of this principle.

When you have everything under control you are in good shape, no matter what you are doing. Learn what you should control in life, and keep in mind that the various ways to go about controlling life are just as important.

Chapter 5

King Safety

The king is the whole game, due to that peculiarity called checkmate. This is what separates chess from all other games or sports. All of the other pieces and pawns are supporting players, that is, helpers. Get the king and it's all over.

So principles relating to king safety have particular merit for chess players. Ignore them and you will fail spectacularly and often.

Principle 19: Castle early and often.
This principle comes in the form of a flip statement. Of course you can only castle once a game, and then only if you have not moved your king or rook previously. But buried in that bit of humor is a deep truth that every good chess player knows about through experience.

If you don't castle early in an open game (this is part of the principle not explicitly stated—your king can often safely stay in the center for quite a while when the game is closed up behind pawn chains), you will be sorry. A game of mine from long ago (Ron Kensek-Kurzdorfer, Buffalo, N.Y., 1976) went:

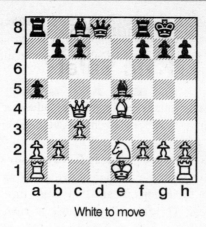

White to move

White spies a combination to win a pawn. But he has not castled. Ignoring that fact, he plays 1. Bxh7+ Kxh7 2. Qe4+ Kg8 3. Qxe5 and only after 3. ... Re8 ...

White to move

does he realize the folly of his combination. He will never get to castle now, as Black pounds on the pinned knight. The game ended 4. Qb5 b6 5. Rd1 Qe7 6. Qd3 Ba6 7. c4 Qb4+ 8. Qc3 Bxc4 9. Rd2 Qb5 10. a4 Qxa4 11. Qc2 Qb5, White resigns.

Every experienced chess player has had something similar happen to him or her—on both sides of the board. We've all won and lost these games due to the failure of one side to castle early enough. Don't be the latest to fall for it!

Protect what is important before going on adventures. You can only leave your home, investments, or loved ones vulnerable at great risk.

Principle 20: Do not move pawns in front of your castled king.
The truth behind this principle is inherent in the way pawns move. Their inability to retrace their steps means that every time a pawn moves, weak squares appear. Therefore, if you move a pawn in front of your king, you are producing weak squares in front of him. An alert opponent will notice those squares and get his pieces trained on them. Thus, you have invited an attack on your monarch. Just what you don't want!

The following position shows a graphic example of leaving the pawns alone in front of a king:

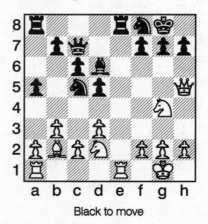

Black to move

Black does well to leave her king in relative safety by relying on his excellent pawn cover. But she is nervous about that queen and decides to expel her. But after 1. ... g6 comes the surprising 2. Nh6 mate!

It may not always be that bad, but you get the picture. Leave the pawns that shelter your king alone.

♟ ♞ ♜ ♛

You've been admonished often enough with "Leave well enough alone." This principle is the chess equivalent. Don't fix what isn't broken. You might just break it by trying to fix it.

Principle 21: Pay particular attention to the f2- and f7-squares.

What are the weakest squares at the beginning of game? The f2- and f7-squares, since they are only protected by the king. Thus, it's a very good idea to be especially wary of combinations aimed at those squares in the early part of the game, especially if the game is taking on an open character.

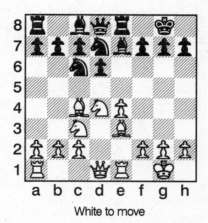

White to move

Black has left the f7-square vulnerable, and White takes advantage with the combination 1. Bxf7+ Kxf7 2. Ne6. Black must give up the queen, getting what she can for it, or suffer an abrupt end of the game after 2. ... Kxe6 3. Qd5+ Kf6 4. Qf5 mate.

♟ ♞ ♜ ♛

Failing to protect what is vulnerable will end in its destruction. Remember that a chain is only as strong as its weakest link. Or, as my conductor used to say, "An orchestra is only as good as its weakest member."

Principle 22: A queen and a rook will always checkmate a naked king.

This is a good principle to know when you have an attack raging and are wondering just how much material you can give up without leaving yourself short of resources.

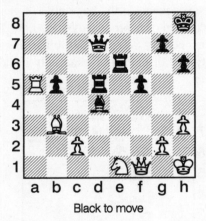

Black to move

Expose that king with 1. ... Rxe1 2. Qxe1 Bc3 3. Qxc3 and now you have what you want. Finish up with 3. ... Rd1+ 4. Kh2 Qd6+ 5. g3. (Of course, you win queen for rook after 5. Qg3 Rh1+. White therefore avoids this, but at a price!) 5. ... Rd2+ 6. Kg1 Qb6+ 7. Kh1 Qb7+ 8. Kg1 Qg2 mate.

When you know precisely how much force will be sufficient, why waste time searching for more? Overkill is never necessary nor particularly efficient. Use what resources you have and be done with it.

Principle 23: **Do not pin your opponent's f3- or f6-knight to his queen with your bishop until after he's castled.**

This principle is very specific, and doesn't really apply in all circumstances. Nevertheless, it has a grain of truth about it, and is meant as a warning against situations like the following (Gilbert-Kurzdorfer, Los Angeles, 1981):

　　1. e4 e5 2. Nf3 Nc6 3. Bc4 Bc5 4. c3 Nf6 5. b4 Bb6 6. d3 d6 7. Bg5

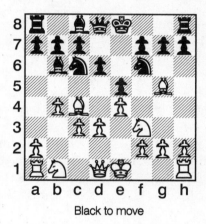

Black to move

White has just pinned the f6-knight to the queen, even though Black is not castled. By not waiting for Black to castle, White allows himself to be pushed back on the kingside:

　　7. ... h6 8. Bh4 Qe7 9. 0-0 Nd8 10. Re1 g5 11. Bg3 h5 12. h4 Bg4

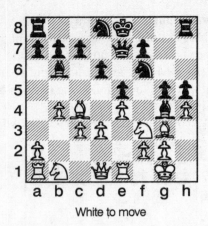

White to move

This pin follows the principle, since White is castled on the kingside.
13. Nbd2

White could get into some wild complications by accepting
Black's pawn sacrifice, but it all turns out to be good for Black after
13. hxg5 h4 14. gxf6 hxg3 15. fxe7 gxf2+ 16. Kf1 Rh1+ 17. Ke2
fxe1=Q+ 18. Qxe1 Rxe1+ 19. Kxe1 Kxe7 and Black has the bishop-
pair and healthier pawns.

13. ... Nh7 14. Qa4+ c6

Black's opening problems were solved, and he eventually won.
Note that White is on the defensive on the kingside, where his king
lives.

♙ ♞ ♜ ♛

An old sports saying states "In order to win, you must first make
sure you don't lose." See to your own (name it) before trying to influ-
ence anyone else's.

Principle 24: Never a mate with a knight on f8.

This principle might be better phrased, rarely a mate with a knight on f8. The f8-knight guards important squares around the Black king after she has castled kingside.

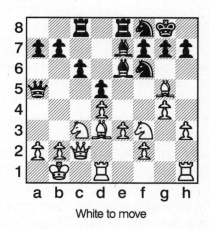

White to move

In this typical Queen's Gambit Declined Exchange Variation, Black is in no immediate danger even though White's pieces are ominously pointing toward her king. That's because Black has plenty of defenders hanging around the kingside and the center, not least of all the knight on f8. Of course, it doesn't hurt that Black has not moved any of the pawns in front of her king either!

The same principle applies to a White knight on f1 guarding a White king on g1, but that doesn't rhyme as well.

♟ ♞ ♜ ♛

It never hurts to have a good, reliable bodyguard. Many people have friends and family who look out for them, and others have dogs or locks to protect them. Don't be caught with nothing or nobody to back you up. It's an unhealthy state.

Chapter 6

Material

It is essential to know the relative value of the various pieces and pawns that occupy the board. They are the major tools you have to work with, and they can be exchanged in many ways. Do you know if three pawns are superior to a knight? Is it better to have a rook and two pawns or a bishop and knight? How about a queen or two rooks? When you know which material is better for the various situations, you are better able to make intelligent decisions on what material to retain and what to give up.

Principle 25: When ahead in material, trade pieces, not pawns.
The reason for this principle lies in the mathematical concept of ratio. An advantage or ten to nine simply isn't as big an advantage as two to one, or better yet, one to nothing. When you have an advantage in material, it makes sense to improve the ratio by trading pieces, but not pawns.

Why not pawns? Very simply, if they all come off the board, you could wind up with a nice, large material advantage of one minor piece to nothing, and no win! A bishop (or knight) and king cannot checkmate a lone king no matter how hard you try. So you will still need some pawns (unless your material advantage is a full rook or better).

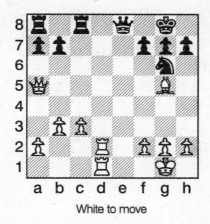

White to move

White is a pawn up. The best way to neutralize any counterplay opportunities for Black is to get as many pieces off the board as possible. Thus, 1. Rd8 Rxd8 2. Rxd8 Rxd8 3. Qxd8 Qxd8 4. Bxd8 gets rid of all the major pieces, and White's task is simplified.

♟ ♞ ♜ ♛

Improve your odds by bettering your ratio. This is a concept that all team sports people know about. It's what makes power-play goals possible in hockey and two-on-one breaks so difficult to defend against in basketball.

Principle 26: When behind in material, trade pawns, not pieces.
This is the flip side of Principle 25. You trade pawns when behind in material to reduce the chance of your opponent promoting a pawn in the endgame. This cannot be done when there are no pawns on the board.

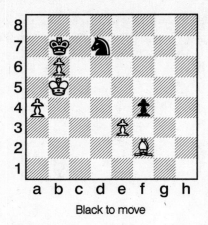

Black to move

Black is down material and has no chance for a counterattack. But she can force a draw with 1. ... fxe3 2. Bxe3 Nxb6 3. Bxb6, and White is left with the wrong bishop for the a-pawn, which cannot successfully promote.

Of course, you have to understand why you are trading pawns in order to know when not to follow this principle. For instance, if you are behind in material but have a terrific initiative, you might simply want to continue your attack, whether it involves trading pawns—or pieces! You may gain the material back with interest or get a checkmating attack going. Who wants to trade pawns then?

As with all the principles, it is best to be aware of the reason behind the principle.

Cut your losses by getting rid of the units that can defeat you. Even if this means you must get rid of the only resources you have left, this is a bargain if you had no chance to win at all in the first place.

Principle 27: In situations with three healthy pawns versus a minor piece, the piece is usually superior in the middlegame, while the pawns are usually superior in the endgame.

Pawns come into their own in the endgame, while pieces, particularly minor pieces, are at their best in the middlegame. This principle can apply equally well to five pawns versus rook, though rooks can be terrors in the endgame if they are placed right.

Don't let this general guideline be a hard-and-fast rule: A lot depends on the pawn structure. Are the pawns connected? Are they passed? Are they broken up into isolated groups, or islands? Are some of them doubled up?

And don't forget the pieces: Are they working well together? Will their range increase or decrease as the endgame draws near? Are there a mixture of bishops and knights, or just two bishops, or two knights? Are rooks still on the board? There are so many factors to take into account in such situations.

A typical case is the end of Kurzdorfer-IM Ed Formanek (Buffalo, 1992):

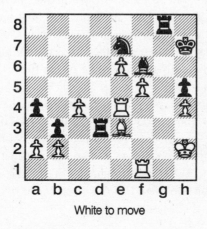

White to move

Black has a knight for the three pawns, which are all passed though not all connected. They are blockaded, and Black is about ready to break through on the queenside. White plays to break the blockade in order to get his pawns moving:

1. Bg5 Rf8 2. axb3 axb3 3. Rf2 Bxg5 4. hxg5 Rxf5 5. Rxf5 Nxf5 6. e7

The blockade is broken, and Black has to surrender his piece to prevent promotion. But he already picked up a pawn and is about to get another pawn on top of the one he sacrifices for, so he winds up giving the piece back for all three pawns.

6. ... Rd2+ 7. Kh3 Nxe7 8. Rxe7+ Kg6 9. Rb7 Rxb2 10. Rb5 and the game ended in a draw.

♟ ♞ ♜ ♛

When comparing objects that are not alike, it's always a good idea to think about what the properties of each are. Although barter isn't practiced as much as it used to be, it's still useful to have a good idea of the value of everything you deal with.

Principle 28: An extra pawn is worth a little trouble.

Of course, you're going to have to figure out, how much trouble is a little? Everybody wants an extra pawn or two (or an extra piece or pieces, for that matter) when all other things are equal. That simply translates to a win well over 95 percent of the time. Other things are seldom that equal.

Trouble often translates into having to defend. So should you be ready to grab that pawn and hunker down? Well, it all depends on the position.

Most opening gambits are of the take-the-pawn-and-have-some-trouble variety. Many are possible to decline, but usually it is better to challenge your opponent. The Marshall Gambit is one of many: 1. e4 e5 2. Nf3 Nc6 3. Bb5 a6 4. Ba4 Nf6 5. 0-0 Be7 6. Re1 b5 7. Bb3 0-0 8. c3 d5.

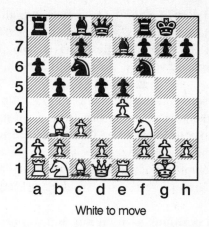

White to move

Most strong players snatch with 9. exd5 Nxd5 10. Nxe5 Nxe5 11. Rxc5 c6 and spend the next few moves defending their ill-gotten gains in the hope of consolidating and winning the endgame. Black's attack after ... Bd6 and ... Qh4 is powerful but not unstoppable. White does have that extra pawn.

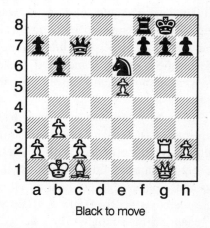

Black to move

On the other hand, it is foolish to snatch the pawn here, since if Black grabs with 1. ... Qxe5 White's attack is more than a little trouble.

After 2. Bb2 Qc7 3. Rxg7+ Nxg7 4. Qxg7 mate ends all argument.

Of course getting a piece is worth even more trouble. But again, how much trouble depends on the position. Grabbing a piece, even a queen, is a bad bargain if you lose the game as a result.

♟ ♞ ♜ ♛

There are all sorts of things that are worth a little trouble: taking the time to mow the lawn or put in that floor, for instance. There are other things worth a lot of trouble: getting a good job or buying a house come to mind. It's up to you to decide how much trouble whatever you are contemplating is worth. Each instance has to be considered on its own merits. There are no easy, all-embracing answers here.

Principle 29: In positions with an unusual disparity in material, the initiative is often the deciding factor.

This is a good guide for many different kinds of positions. For example, rook and two pawns against bishop and knight; queen and pawn versus two rooks; rook, knight, and two pawns versus queen, and so on. When in doubt, play for the initiative. If you are calling the shots, it's very hard for your opponent to organize a winning plan against you.

The following position came up in Kurzdorfer-GM Dmitry Gurevich in Washington, D.C., in 1990. White has rook and pawn for two knights, the g5-bishop is en prise, and the d7-bishop is pinned to Black's rook. It is White's move, and I moved the hanging bishop to f4, sensibly enough.

This turned out to be good enough for a draw (after some hair-raising complications), but if I had paid more attention to Principle 29, I might have done better. With 1. Bh3 Bxh3 2. Rxe7 fxg5 3. Rxb5, we get an unusual situation with two rooks and two pawns against four minor pieces. It's not hard to tell who has the initiative, since White threatens 4. Rb8+ Bf8 5. Re8, winning a piece, along with 4. Ra7, snaring both knights for a rook. These are hard threats for Black to deal with.

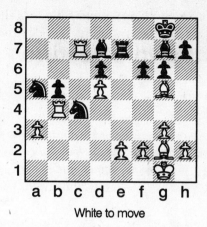

White to move

There are many ways to take charge of a situation. Some of these cost more trouble. So do a cost analysis, and find out if what you are paying is balanced by the control you are getting. You will find that often the price isn't as high as it might at first appear.

Chapter 7

Pawn Structure

"The passed pawn is a criminal, who should be kept under lock and key. Mild measures, such as police surveillance, are not sufficient."
—Aron Nimzovich, *My System*

The pawn structure provides the clues to any possible future plans. This is because of the peculiar weakness of the pawn; it cannot move backward or sideways. So pawns have a tendency to stay put, either finding ways to protect each other or their pieces or waiting patiently for the opportunity to protect each other or their pieces.

Pieces, on the other hand, can retrace their steps, so any piece structure that you might play for is strictly temporary, unless such a structure takes the pawn skeleton into consideration.

Principle 30: Passed pawns must be pushed.

The passed pawn has a lust to expand, as Aron Nimzovich put it. This is simply because every step it takes brings it closer to promotion, and that means a huge increase in strength. Most other pawns aren't so eager to move forward.

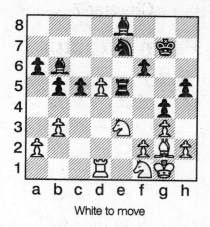

White to move

Just look at that lusty fellow on d5. The next few moves are not very hard to figure out: 1. d6 Ng6 2. d7 Bf7 3. d8=Q and Black must give up a piece for the new queen with 3. ... Bxd8 4. Rxd8. Other variations wind up the same way. Black must surrender a piece for the passed pawn.

Forge ahead when you have a clearly definable goal in sight.

Principle 31: Doubled pawns are a weakness in that they are immobile, but a strength in that they offer half-open files for rooks.

This principle simply states the major strength and weakness of doubled pawns. They have other strengths—such as the extra squares they command along either file, and other weaknesses—such as the inability to defend each other. Your task, when contemplating whether to accept doubled pawns or to inflict them on your opponent, or how to deal with them now that they have appeared, is to make the most of your strengths and your opponent's weaknesses.

A famous example of doubled pawns is the Nimzo-Indian Defense, where after 1. d4 Nf6 2. c4 e6 3. Nc3 Bb4 4. a3 Bxc3 5. bxc3

White accepts doubled c-pawns in order to strengthen his center. He also gets the use of the half-open b-file, while Black gave up the bishop-pair.

Black to move

Black will often play 5. ... c5 in order to make sure the doubled pawns remain where they are—ripe for attack. The entire game will often revolve around White trying to prove the doubled pawns are strong while Black attempts to prove they are weak.

♟ ♞ ♜ ♛

Strengths and weaknesses are inherent in many things; perhaps they are inherent in everything. That's one of the unifying ideas of Chinese philosophy with its yin and yang, or opposite sides of any conceivable thing or idea. It finds full expression here in the Jekyll and Hyde of doubled pawns.

Principle 32: Look to liquidate backward and isolated pawns.
The trouble with backward and isolated pawns is that, by definition, they can have no pawn support. Therefore, if you want to hold on to them, you must defend them with pieces. But pieces have better things to do than hold on to weak pawns.

Often the best way out of this dilemma is to just get rid of the offensive weakling. As a bonus, you will gain open diagonals for bishops and open files or ranks for rooks. And you may even pick up a nice outpost square for a knight in the process.

White to move

In this position, White's bishop is under attack, and he has an isolated d-pawn. The bishop could retreat safely enough, but why not take care of the problem of the isolated pawn? This works especially well here, since White has more pieces in play.

1. d5 exd5 2. Bxd5 Nxd5 3. Qxd5 Bxg5 4. Qxc6 Bg4 5. Ne5 Be6 6. Rad1

White's pieces are all in play on nice, open lines, while Black has yet to bring his rooks into the game. He can't even do that yet, since his queen is under attack (Kurzdorfer-Harvey Selib, Buffalo, 1987).

Liquidating liabilities is an old strategy in business, and I suspect in a lot of things. If you can also gain strength for your remaining assets while getting rid of your weakness, by all means, go for it.

Principle 33: Fewer pawn islands means a healthier position.

Pawn islands are groups of pawns that are connected to each other in some way and have the ability to defend each other. The ability to

defend each other makes them healthy. If pawns do not require piece
support, the pieces are free to go off on adventures without having to
worry about defending stray pawns.

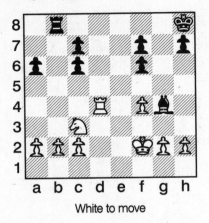

White to move

This position (from a 1978 game in Philadelphia, Alex Dunne-
Kurzdorfer) shows the stark contrast between healthy and unhealthy
pawns. Black's little guys cannot call on each other for defense. Each
has to look out for himself. Thus, Black's pieces will be tied to the
defense of the pawns, unless he wants to give them all up. White, on
the other hand, has two healthy pawn islands, where each pawn can
call on the others for assistance. This frees up the White pieces for
other things, such as attacking the Black pawns.

♟ ♞ ♜ ♛

The less you need to tie up precious resources for menial tasks,
the more you will be able to take advantage of opportunities that come
your way. This is why executives of all sorts have secretaries—to get
the mundane, day-to-day chores taken care of so the boss can function
on a higher level. Those who must take on all the detail work themselves simply don't function as well.

Principle 34: If you must accept pawn weaknesses, make sure you get compensation in one form or another.

Accepting a weak pawn or weak pawns may be a necessary price you are willing to pay for some sort of gain. Just make sure you get something in return, or you will wind up with nothing but liabilities.

Compensation can take all sorts of forms. Gaining the bishop pair versus bishop and knight, taking the initiative, winning a pawn, gaining a strong square for your knight, and gaining control of the center are all types of compensation that may make your weak pawns bearable. But each instance has to be weighed on its own merit in the given position. How much compensation is enough for whatever pawn weakness you are left with is a question that can't be answered in a general way.

One example of compensation is the free play for the pieces and strong center Black gets in the Tarrasch Variation of the Queen's Gambit Declined for his isolated d-pawn after 1. d4 d5 2. c4 e6 3. Nc3 c5 4. cxd5 exd5 5. Nf3 Nc6 6. g3 Nf6 7. Bg2 Be7 8. 0-0 0-0 9. Bg5 cxd4 10. Nxd4 h6 11. Be3 Re8.

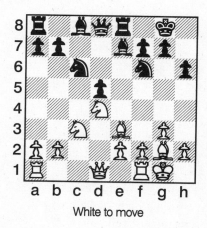

White to move

Whether this is enough compensation for the isolated pawn is an open question. But there is no question about accepting such a weakness without compensation of any sort.

♟ ♞ ♜ ♛

Don't give anything away without at least getting something in return. Any weakness or poor position you accept has to be accompanied by some compensating strength or good position elsewhere. Otherwise you have nothing but a losing proposition.

Chapter 8

Space

"A cramped position contains the seeds of defeat."
—Siegbert Tarrasch

The territory you control is an important factor in assessing any position. Gaining control of more squares than your opponent has is an advantage, all other things being equal.

Principle 35: Location, location, location.

Ask any real estate agent "what are the three most important aspects of real estate?" and she'll probably answer: location, location, location.

The same holds true for chess. The chessboard is filled with real estate: prime, mediocre, and poor. The location of the kings is paramount, but the location of every piece and pawn also carries importance to varying degrees.

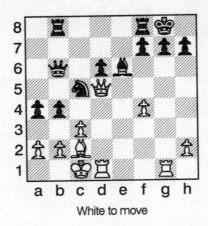

White to move

Black has more pieces and pawns, but her king is in a vulnerable location and the White pieces are poised to take advantage, controlling the half-open g-file and b1-h7 diagonal as well as the open 5th rank. Thus the games ends abruptly after 1. Rxg7+ Kxg7 2. Qg5+ Kh8 3. Qf6+ Kg8 4. Rg1+ Bg4 5. Rxg4 mate.

Real estate professionals understand this principle about as well as anyone. Your location in relation to anyone or anything you are dealing with is of prime importance.

Your location is your focal point. Your home is your focal point for many activities. At work, your office may be your focal point. Wherever you are can have a big impact on what you do and when you do it.

Those who play or watch team sports such as football, basketball, hockey, or baseball know that the location of each player on the field is of critical importance. This principle is no different in a board game.

Principle 36: Exchange pieces to free your game when cramped.
Cramped positions are bad because the pieces have nowhere to go. They need places to go and pieces and pawns to see in order to be

happy. So simply get a few of them off the board, and those that are left will have somewhere to go.

A good example of this principle is the following equalizing attempt in the old Queen's Gambit Declined.

1. d4 d5 2. c4 e6 3. Nc3 Nf6 4. Bg5 Be7 5. e3 0-0 6. Nf3 Nbd7 7. Rc1 c6 8. Bd3

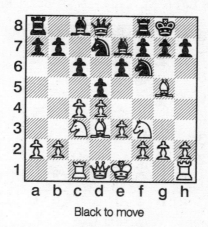

Black to move

Black is cramped for space; her pieces don't have a lot of room to maneuver around. So she begins a policy of exchanging some pieces, and winds up with 8. ... dxc4 9. Bxc4 Nd5 10. Bxe7 Qxe7 11. 0-0 Nxc3 12. Rxc3 e5 13. dxe5 Nxe5 14. Nxe5 Qxe5, after which her remaining pieces have plenty of room to roam.

Not too many people will thrive in a stultifying atmosphere. We must have room to think and grow; room to move about. If your space becomes cramped, you may want to do something to relieve it, such as clearing out some of the dead wood—whatever that may be and however you might want to clear it out.

Principle 37: Avoid piece exchanges when you control more squares.
This principle is the mirror of Principle 36. Since exchanging pieces
relieves a cramp, how do you keep your opponent cramped? Why, by
avoiding such exchanges, of course.

For instance, in the Ruy Lopez, after 1. e4 e5 2. Nf3 Nc6 3. Bb5
Nf6 4. 0-0 d6 5. d4 Bd7 6. Nc3 exd4 7. Nxd4 Be7 8. Re1 0-0.

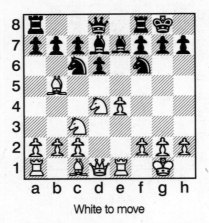

White to move

White can avoid exchanging several sets of minor pieces by
playing 9. Bf1 (or even 9. Nde2), since Black is cramped for space.

Keep control of a situation by not allowing comfortable outlets for
others. It's another oldie but goodie.

**Principle 38: Break a bind in order to free your pieces, even if it
costs a pawn.**
It is essential to break a bind in which your pieces cannot operate, or
you will be smothered to death. So find a way to break such a bind
whenever you find yourself in one. If there is a price to pay, pay it!

In the Sicilian Defense, after 1. e4 c5 2. Nf3 d6 3. d4 cxd4 4.
Nxd4 Nf6 5. Nc3 Nc6 6. Bg5 e6 7. Qd2 Be7 8. 0-0-0 0-0 9. f4.

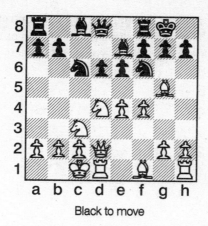

Black to move

Black is short on squares for her pieces. So she offers to trade minor pieces (Principle 36), and pitches a pawn in order to give her remaining pieces more life with 9. ... h6 10. Bxf6 Bxf6 11. Nxc6 bxc6 12. Qxd6 Qb6 13. Qd3 Rb8 14. b3 Rd8. This position is considered equal.

♟ ♞ ♜ ♛

Do whatever it takes to get your goals accomplished. If it involves a cost that's not overwhelming, pay it. Your goal is important, after all.

Principle 39: The move ... d7-d5 is the antidote for the poison in many gambits.

At times, this principle is a specific expression of Principle 38, but it also embodies some principles you will run into later.

The main idea behind this guideline is that after playing a gambit, White has more pieces in play and more central control (if he doesn't, his gambit was bad to begin with). The move ... d7-d5 will often serve to rectify that state of affairs, since it places a pawn in an important central square, very likely attacking something, while opening up lines of development for Black's queen and light-square bishop.

A case in point is the Danish Gambit where after 1. e4 e5 2. d4 exd4 3. c3 dxc3 4. Bc4 cxb2 5. Bxb2.

after 5. Bxb2

White has given up three pawns, but has much better development and central control. A good reaction by Black is the combination 5. ... d5 6. Bxd5 Nf6 7. Bxf7+ Kxf7 8. Qxd8 Bb4+ 9. Qd2 Bxd2+ 10. Nxd2 Re8, when Black has given back the pawns but caught up in development and central control.

In fact, in a broader sense, the move ... d7-d5 is often an equalizing move even when White has not given up a pawn. Take, for example, the Giuoco Piano after 1. e4 e5 2. Nf3 Nc6 3. Bc4 Bc5 4. c3 Nf6 5. d4 exd4 6. cxd4 Bb4+ 7. Bd2 Bxd2+ 8. Nbxd2.

after 8. Nbxd2

Black's best move is considered 8. ... d5, which equalizes nicely.

If you fall behind in something that is important, catch up. Make catching up a top priority or you may never catch up at all.

Chapter 9

Tempo

The move is your major weapon. Use it wisely.

Tempo refers to the unit of the move in chess, to distinguish it from using time in the sense of the amount of time a move, a series of moves, or an entire game takes. Thus tempo is time in a purely chess sense.

Principle 40: Don't attack unless you have the superior game.

You could make an attacking move every time it is your turn. But doing so will not work very often. There are other considerations to take into account. Attacking before you are ready to attack will likely backfire, since your opponent will likely be ready for anything you can throw at him.

This principle is a warning to be prepared before launching an attack. On a deeper level, it embraces the concept of being prepared for any action you may want to take at all, which includes defensive, evasive, or preventive action as well as attacking action. The main idea is to first be prepared.

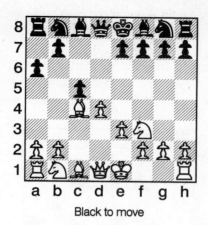

Black to move

In this position (Kurzdorfer-Lee Travers, N. Tonawanda, NY, 1987), a fairly strong competitor actually played 1. ... b5. Of course he lost soon after 2. Bxf7+ Kxf7 3. Ne5+ with a devastating attack.

Mr. Travers wanted to attack so badly he forgot to look at the position. A simple glance is enough to convince anybody that Black is in no position to attack. He is far behind in development and has no central control at all. Therefore a modest move such as 1. ... Nf6 or 1. ... e6 is called for. These moves aren't world shattering, but they will keep Black alive so that he may be able to attack at a later time.

♟ ♞ ♜ ♛

The Boy Scouts of America's motto is "Be prepared." This is good advice for everybody, including chess players. Performing on stage when you have not practiced will produce a poor, embarrassing performance. Attacking a well-prepared opponent on the fly will rarely work in any sport or game.

Principle 41: You must attack when you have the superior game, or you will forfeit your advantage.

This guide takes Principle 40 a step further. It isn't enough to be prepared before you attack. You then must follow up and attack. To fail to attack when you are in position to do so will result in losing your advantage. Both principles come from World Chess Champion Emanuel Lasker.

This puts a slightly different spin on the idea of having an advantage. It places the player with the better game in a stressful situation. The pressure is on, since you now must act, or lose your advantage.

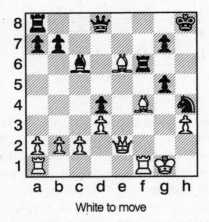

White to move

White has an advantage with the bishop pair, well-placed major pieces, and an exposed Black king. But this advantage has to be cashed in now, or White will be in trouble, since his king is also exposed. Capturing on g5 loses the bishop to 1. Bxg5 Rxf1+ 2. Rxf1 Qxg5, while moving the threatened bishop to other squares allows the powerful 1. ... Nf3+. But if White calculates accurately, he will find the winning 1. Qh5+ Rh6 2. Qxh6+ gxh6 3. Be5+ Kh7 4. Rf7+ Kg6 (or 4. ... Kg8 5. Rc7+ Kf8 6. Bg7+ Ke8 7. Bf7 mate) 5. Rg7+ Kh5 6. Bg4 mate.

She who hesitates is lost. There's no room in this life for indecision. Once you are on the road to better things, don't loiter; get the job done. Otherwise you could find yourself on another road altogether.

Principle 42: Every move is an opportunity to interfere with your opponent's plans, or to further your own plans.

Improving a piece or denying your opponent a square won't win the game for you, but doing many of these things each move will eventually pile up, and you will be in a great position to win.

Each move is precious; don't waste even one.

Principle 43: A sustained initiative is worth some material.

For how long should you sustain the initiative? and How much material is 'some'? There really is no answer to the first question in terms of number of moves, but rather in what concessions your opponent will have to give in order to bring your initiative to a halt. Generally, the longer your initiative lasts, the more concessions it will take to break it. As for the second question, that all depends on how lasting the initiative is. Is this circular thinking? Perhaps, but there's simply no way to consider either factor in isolation reliably.

Here is an example in which the initiative is easily enough to justify the sacrifice of a bishop:

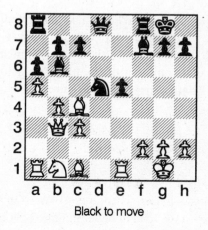

Black to move

   After 1. ... Bxf2+ 2. Kxf2 Qh4+ 3. Ke2 Nxc3+ 4. Qxc3 Bxc4+ 5.
Kd1 Rad8+ Black has two pawns for the piece, as well as open lines
for his pieces, a big lead in development, and a very exposed White
king to work against. White is in trouble in anybody's book (Jonathan
Yedidia-Kurzdorfer, Philadelphia, 1979).

♟ ♞ ♜ ♛

   Weigh the consequences of any investment you make. After getting some experience, you will soon get the feeling of how much is
acceptable to give up and how much is too much.

**Principle 44: The initiative is an advantage. Take it whenever
you can, and take it back when you don't have it, if at all possible.**
Among better players it is considered an advantage to begin the game
with the White pieces. Why? Simply because White moves first. This
gives the first player the first chance to take the initiative. Perhaps this
isn't as much of an advantage as having the serve in tennis, but it is close.

   With the initiative, you can force the play into channels of your
choosing. You can impose your will on the position. This is not an
advantage to lightly give up.

   In the following position, White thinks the initiative is so important he gives up a whole rook for it. Whether he was ultimately right
or not can only be discovered by a thorough examination of the multiple possibilities that come out of the play that actually took place
(Kurzdorfer-David Hart, correspondence game, 1981):

White to move

1. Bg5 f6 2. exf6 gxf6 3. Ne3 Nxa1 4. Nxf5 fxg5

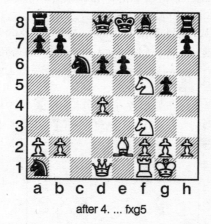

after 4. ... fxg5

Down a rook, White plays to open lines:

5. d5 exf5 6. dxc6 bxc6 7. Qd4 Rg8 8. Qc4 Rg6 9. Qxc6+ Ke7 10. Qb7+ Kf6

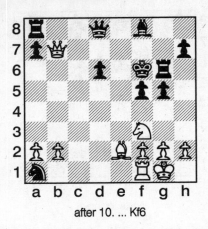

after 10. ... Kf6

Now White begins threatening checkmate while bringing more pieces in play.

11. Bc4 Rg7 12. Qd5 Re7 13. Nd4 Qc8 14. Qxd6+ Kg7 15. Qd5 Rc7 16. Nxf5+ Kg6 17. Nd6 Qd8 18. Qe6+, Black resigns.

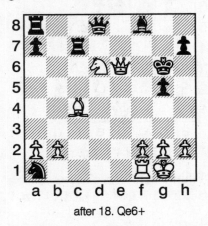

after 18. Qe6+

In the final position, White is still down a rook for two pawns, but Black is getting checkmated.

Whether in business, sports, politics, or any other aspect of a highly competitive life, taking and keeping the initiative is the best way to impose your will on anything.

Chapter 10
Mobility

Give your pieces and pawns somewhere to go and something to do. Bishops, knights, rooks, queens, and even kings were made to move, not to be blocked up with nowhere to go and nobody to see.

Principle 45:

> *"A rook on the seventh rank is sufficient*
> *compensation for a pawn."*
>   —Reuben Fine

This principle shows the power of the rook on a half-open rank in the enemy territory in very specific terms. Such a rook has good mobility, and in this case that can be measured in terms of pawns. Thus having such a mobile rook (on the seventh rank for a White rook or on the second rank for a Black rook—in other words, the seventh rank counting from the rank where all your pieces start out) is equivalent to having an extra pawn. This is a good bit of advice to know any time you have a chance to gain entry into your opponent's position.

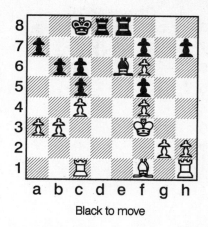

Black to move

Black has the game under control. His rooks can reach and main-tain the second rank, while White's f6-pawn is weak. After 1. ... Rd2 2. h3 Bd7 3. g3 Re6 4. Rb1 Rxf6, Black still controls the second rank, so he is in effect a pawn up. He eventually won (Deep Fritz-GM Garry Kasparov, Bahrain, 2002).

The basketball guard who has fast feet, quick hands, and control of the ball by dribbling and precision passing is valuable to his team. These abilities are often sufficient compensation for his lack of height. Mobility is sometimes a desirable asset that can be measured in terms of other assets.

Principle 46: Superior development increases in value in propor-tion to the openness of the game.
The more open the game, the more important piece development is. You can fall behind in development, even avoid castling for a long time, quite safely if the position is locked behind pawn chains. But if the pawns clear out and there is lots of room to maneuver for the pieces, you better get your pieces in the thick of the action quickly.

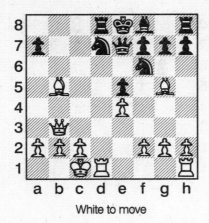

White to move

1. Rxd7 Rxd7 2. Rd1 Qe6 3. Bxd7+ Nxd7 4. Qb8+ Nxb8 5. Rd8 mate. This may well be the most famous game of all time (Paul Morphy-Duke of Brunswick/Count Isouard, Paris, 1858). The final combination should have come as no surprise, since White has a huge lead in development, while the position is very open.

This is another ratio principle. The more room there is to maneuver, the more it matters that there are pieces available to use that room.

♟ ♞ ♜ ♛

When there are more lines of communication available, it makes sense to use them. Those who stick to the old letter-in-the-mailbox route are going to be left behind in our age of telephone, fax, and e-mail.

Principle 47: Attacking two weaknesses on opposite sides of the board simultaneously will stretch out the defense.
This is the old principle of double attack. With a greater area to defend, the defender has to stretch his resources.

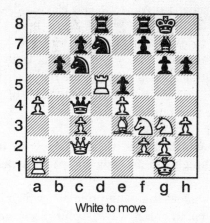

White to move

White sets up a double battery with the move 1. Qd2. Black has to find a way to defend h6 and d7 simultaneously. This proved awkward, if not impossible after 1. ... Ndb8 2. Bxh6 Rxd5 3. exd5 Rd8 4. Bxg7 Kxg7.

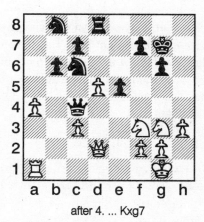

after 4. ... Kxg7

Black will win back the extra d5-pawn, but not until his king is exposed after 5. Nf5+ gxf5 6. Qg5+ Kf8 7. dxc6 Rd5 8. Qxf5 Nxc6 9. Re1 Qxc3 10. Re4. White went on to win with his great superiority in force on the kingside (Kurzdorfer-Keith Haywood, correspondence game, 1978).

♟ ♞ ♜ ♛

Tire your opponent by giving him many tasks to do. In football, the offense will sustain a long drive to tire the other team's defense. Tennis players will hit the ball to opposite sides of the court every other stroke to tire their opponents.

Principle 48: The bishop pair is usually superior to a bishop and a knight or two knights in an endgame with pawns on both sides of the board.

This is a very technical-sounding principle, which can perhaps be better stated in a nontechnical way. If your pieces can cover all the available squares in a hurry, you are in a better position than if they can only cover some of the squares, or can cover them all, but only very slowly. The two bishops can indeed cover all the squares of the board in a hurry, provided one or both aren't hemmed in or tied down to defense.

The following position may seem an odd choice to prove that the bishop pair is superior to the knight pair. But if you understand the reasoning behind the principle, you will have no trouble understanding why White is better, even though it is his knight pair that does the job usually accorded the bishop pair.

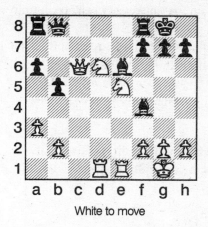

White to move

White has more pieces developed in an open position (Principle 46) and controls the center by occupying it with pieces (Principle 16), so it should come as no surprise that he is better. The play went 1. g3 Bxe5 2. Rxe5 Rd8 3. Ree1 Ra7 4. Ne4 Rad7 5. Rxd7 Bxd7 6. Qxa6. White won a pawn, while retaining all his other advantages (Kurzdorfer-Harvey Selib, Buffalo, 1987).

Covering a large area thoroughly and swiftly is generally going to bring greater rewards than covering some of the area or covering all of it slowly.

Principle 49: Opposite-colored bishops will usually give the weaker player a good chance to draw a bishop-and-pawn endgame, but can often be a virtual extra piece for the attacker in a middlegame.

This is another technical principle that covers a greater truth. Opposite-colored bishops are distinctive because each controls squares the other cannot reach. If these are the only pieces left on the board, each one will be unable to cover the squares it does not control. Therefore, the side with fewer pawns merely needs to blockade the opponent's pawns on the squares her bishop controls, and no progress can be made.

Of course, things aren't always so simple. If the pawns are connected or if one king is active while the other is far from the action, the outcome could change.

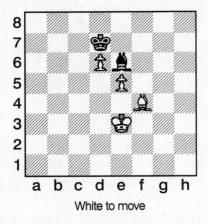

White to move

Black is two pawns down, yet has no trouble holding the draw. He merely shuffles his bishop around, and as long as he is careful to hang on to it and make sure it is always covering e6, the game will end in a draw.

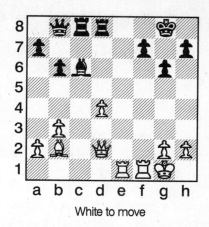

White to move

White has no trouble winning here, simply pitching the d-pawn with 1. d5. There is no way for Black to stop the White queen from getting to c3, d4, or h6, all of which threaten mate at g7 with the unleashed b2-bishop.

♟ ♞ ♜ ♛

When you have an equal number of uncompromising voters on opposite sides of an issue, it will not get resolved. When a politician runs unopposed for a position, she will get in. You have to take into account not only the issue or the politician, but also the situation they find themselves in. Issues, people, or tools of any kind are not intrinsically useful. But they can be situationally useful. These are truths we all know.

Chapter 11

Tactics

"Chess is 99% tactics."
—Richard Teichmann

*"The scheme of a game is played on positional lines;
the decision of it, as a rule, is effected by combinations."*
—Richard Reti

Tactics are the immediate, forcing moves that disturb the balance of a position in any way. They include surprise moves, captures, promotions, checks, and moves that threaten to capture, promote, or check.

Principle 50: Don't grab the b-pawn with your queen—even when it's good!

It may seem strange to admonish you to stay away from a course of action even when it is good, but there's a grain of truth in this slightly absurd saying. There are many examples in which one side took the bait, and then regretted it. Capturing the b-pawn with your queen will often put her majesty out of play and far from the action. But surely it will be all right when there is a clear way for her to get back into the action in plenty of time.

The trouble is that such a clear plan is not often easy to implement. So, rather than clinging slavishly to this admonition, take a close, critical look at the position and assess the ramifications of the grab. Check your analysis again. Chances are your concept isn't so good, but you may have stumbled on a rare exception in this case. If so, grab the little guy and run with your gain.

There is actually a respected opening variation in which Black ignores this principle, but I don't suggest using it with either side unless you have made a special study of it, since the theory on it is extremely complicated. It is the famous Poison Pawn Variation of the Sicilian Defense, popularized by World Champion Bobby Fischer before and during his 1972 championship match with Boris Spassky in Reykjavik, Iceland. It begins 1. e4 c5 2. Nf3 d6 3. d4 cxd4 4. Nxd4 Nf6 5. Nc3 a6 6. Bg5 e6 7. f4 Qb6 8. Qd2 Qxb2.

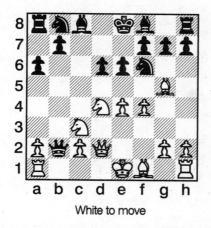

White to move

If you play this line without doing any home analysis, you will likely learn about how much more important memory is than anything else. But you will also notice that White has quite an initiative, and you will only enjoy playing Black if you are comfortable defending for a long time.

For the most part, follow generally accepted advice. But if you are not going to follow it, make sure you know what you're doing. There are good, sound reasons that this advice is generally accepted.

Principle 51: The double attack is the principle behind almost all tactics.

This principle involves simple logic. An attack on two or more objects is harder to meet than an attack on only one. There is more for your opponent to take into consideration; therefore the likelihood of her making a mistake goes up. Even if she doesn't make a mistake, the energy she spends on the solution to the problem may tire her for later in the game.

Since every other move in master chess is a double attack of some sort, my example is something a little rarer: a fourfold attack.

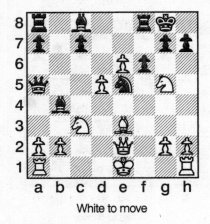

White to move

Black has just moved the queen from b6, where it was under attack, to a5. This move created four threats. The first is the simple 1. ... fxg5, winning the knight. The second is the sneaky 1. ... Qxd5, picking up a free pawn because of the pin on the c3-knight. The third is the combination 1. ... Bxc3+ 2. bxc3 Qxc3+, winning a pawn. The fourth is the combination 1. ... Ba6 2. Qd2 Nd3+ 3. Kd1 Nxb2+. White, not surprisingly, could not defend them all and succumbed after 1. 0-0 Ba6 2. Qh5 fxg5 3. Rxf8+ Rxf8 (Glen Gratz-Kurzdorfer, Chicago, 1992).

The more problems you can create for an opponent simultaneously, the harder it is for her to take care of all of them. Therefore, keep her busy with as many problems as you can.

Principle 52: Ignore your opponent's threats whenever you can do so with impunity.

This principle has a great psychological effect. When your opponent has threatened you, he expects you to do something about the threat. When you don't, and he notices that carrying out his threat won't hurt you at all, it makes him question his judgment about making the threat in the first place.

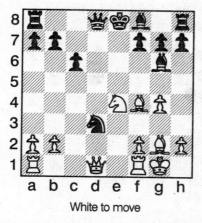

White to move

White's f4-bishop is under fire. The Black knight just moved from e5, where it was under fire from the bishop, in order to force the bishop to move again. But the bishop doesn't move. Instead, we get 1. Qe2, and Black has to take a second look at his last move. Carrying out his threat loses instantly to 1. Nxf4 Nf6 mate. Meanwhile, White threatens 2. Rad1, pinning and winning the knight. This little series of moves turned the game around, and White soon won (Kurzdorfer-John Stopa, Buffalo, 1990).

When you have a chance to make your opponent reassess what he has done, it's often worthwhile to do so. Meanwhile, you can make inroads, improving your position in ways your opponent meant to prevent.

Principle 53: Doubled rooks have more than twice the power of one rook.

This principle may seem hard to believe at first glance, but it is often true. This is another related principle: The bishop pair is also more than twice as strong as one bishop alone, but that's not so hard to grasp. After all, bishops by themselves can only control half the squares on the board.

This principle relates to the exceptional power of batteries. The rook behind adds to the power of the rook in front, and the two together are very hard to resist.

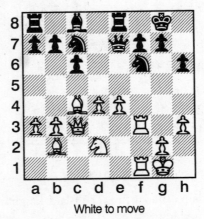

White to move

White commands the f-file with his doubled rooks, and uses them to destroy Black's king with 1. d5 cxd5 2. Rxf6 gxf6 3. Qg3+ Kh7 4. Rxf6 Rg8 5. Qf4 Rg7 6. Rxh6+ Kg8 7. Rh8+, Black resigns.

There is no stopping 7. ... Kxh8 8. Qh6+ Kg8 9. Qxg7 mate (Dusko Prelevic-Dordijevic, 2000).

The total is frequently greater than the sum of the parts.

Principle 54: Hit 'em where they ain't.

If your opponent has an offside piece or an undeveloped piece, attack on the other side of the board. This is nothing more than common sense.

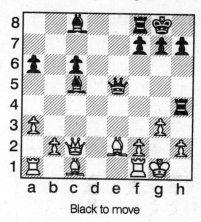

Black to move

White's rook on a1 is not participating in any way. So Black forges ahead with a kingside attack, where he has more pieces and an exposed White king to contend with.

1. ... Bh3

This move also follows Principle 52: the h4-rook is in no danger, since 2. gxh4 is met by 2. ... Qd5.

2. Rd1 Re4 3. Bf1 Re1 4. Rxe1 Qxe1 5. Qe2 Re8 6. Bd2 Qxe2, Black resigns.

His out-of-play rook is finally ready to enter the game, but it is too late, since Black is now a piece down (Neil Goldberg-Kurzdorfer, Buffalo, 1984).

Sports players are well aware of this principle. The running back in a football game finds a hole that his linemen have created and scoots through where there are no defenders. The basketball three-on-one break results in a basket. The insurance goal in hockey goes into an empty net. The tennis player makes a point by hitting the ball to an area her opponent is running away from. Relying on this principle created all these scenarios.

Principle 55: Relentlessly attack pinned pieces, weak pawns, exposed kings, and other immobile targets.

Go after anything that cannot move. Hit it and hit it again. If this seems harsh, it is. But we do not play chess in order to be nice to our opponents. We play to win the game.

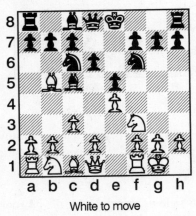

White to move

The knight at c6 is immobile. It cannot move. Therefore, White wants to attack it, and does so by 1. d4 exd4 2. cxd4 Bb6 (or 2. ... Bb4 3. d5 a6 4. Qa4) 3. d5.

Stationary objects are the easiest to hit, therefore nail them down and hit them. It may not be pretty, but it is effective and saves a lot of effort.

Chapter 12

Forcing Moves

"The pin is mightier than the sword."

—Fred Reinfeld

Captures, checks, promotions, and threats to capture, check, or promote demand an immediate response. If these threats are carried out, the balance of the game is tipped in favor of the one capturing, checking, or promoting. Therefore, such forcing moves are powerful weapons indeed.

Principle 56: **The threat you do not see is the one that will defeat you.**

Know what is being threatened at all times. There is no room for inattention to detail in a chess game, not if you want to play a reasonable game.

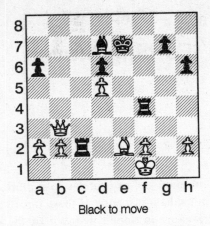

Black to move

Black saw the threat 2. Qxc2 and so played 1. ... Ba4. After 2.
Qe3+, he resigned. It really shouldn't have been too difficult to see
that there were two threats, and that 2. Qe3+ was one of them. It is,
after all, a check. Of course, 1. ... Bf5 (2. Qe3+ Re4) takes care of both
threats, but in order to find the move, Black has to see both threats
(Michael Petras-Kurzdorfer, Buffalo, 1990).

♟ ♞ ♜ ♛

Always pay attention to the little details. Missing one can have
catastrophic repercussions, and you never know when or where that
may happen.

Principle 57: Always check, it might be mate!

This is actually a bit of bad advice with a tiny grain of truth to it. If
your opponent is in check, there is only a limited amount of damage
he can inflict on you. On the other hand, the check should be a pur-
poseful move, aimed at gaining something, just like any other move.
A check played just for the sake of putting a scare into the opposing
king is, at best, silly and, at worst, can ruin your game.

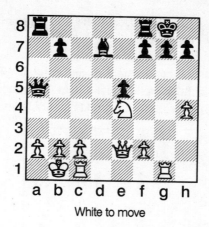

White to move

White should defend the checkmate threat at a2, probably with 1. a3. If he succumbs to the temptation to check instead, he loses a piece after 1. Nf6+ Kh8, when he still has to defend against the checkmate threat, thus abandoning the knight.

♟ ♞ ♜ ♛

All that glitters is not gold, and all checks aren't necessarily good.

Principle 58: Never miss a check!

All checks may not necessarily be good (Principle 57), but don't let that stop you from noticing every possible check at all times during any chess game. How else can you assess whether the check is good, unless you can foresee them all? See the figure on page 80 again for the consequences of missing a potential check. The king is the whole game, after all.

♟ ♞ ♜ ♛

Don't get so caught up in myriad details and minutiae that you miss the most important detail of all. Always be aware of the big picture.

Principle 59: Be aware of the numbers and types of attackers and defenders in a convergence.

Count the number of attackers and defenders of any key square. That square is safe if the number of attackers and defenders is the same, and lost if the number of attackers is greater than the number of defenders, provided the type of pieces attacking and defending are the same.

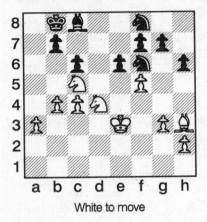

White to move

The count is four to three on e6. Therefore, White wins e6 with 1. fxe6 fxe6 2. Bxe6 Nxe6 3. Ncxe6 Bxe6 4. Nxe6. Of course, if the type of piece isn't the same, such a simple count isn't applicable:

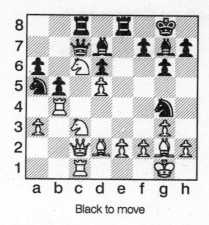

Black to move

This one is different. The count is four to two on c6, but Black can't simply win a pawn, since one of the attackers is the d7-bishop, which is also needed to defend the knight on g4. Thus 1. ... Nxc6 2. dxc6 Bxc6 3. Rxg4.

Furthermore, in each position, there are other things going on after all the exchanges on the key squares. In the first figure on page 82, Black has a check on g4, although g7 is also hanging, while in the second figure, Black can play 3. ... Rxe2 with a pin on the d2-bishop at the end of the exchanges. The count in a convergence is thus only one factor among many.

Don't forget to count up your assets and liabilities. At least be aware of whether you are ahead or behind at any given time. This won't give you the whole picture, but will provide you with a starting point.

Chapter 13

Sacrifice

"To free your game, take off some of your adversary's men, if possible for nothing."
—Captain Bertin from *The Noble Game of Chess* (1735)

A correct sacrifice is no sacrifice at all. Rather, it is an investment, giving up one thing to obtain something of greater value later on.

Principle 60: Sacrifice your opponent's pieces.
This principle is almost too silly to state. Yet sometimes players will forget that, everything else being equal, greater material will prevail over lesser material. Don't be guilty of such forgetfulness.

If you have a chance to go after material, don't be afraid of it. Yes, you might come under attack for a while, but remember Principle 28—an extra pawn is worth a little trouble.

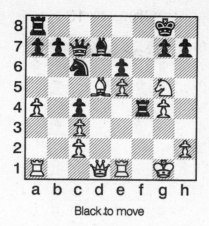

Black to move

White has just played the surprise piece sacrifice 1. Bxd5, picking off a pawn. Black could get the pawn back and maintain a nice central position with 1. ... Nxe5, but why not make White prove he has something for the piece? After 1. ... exd5 2. Qxd5+ Kh8 3. Nf7+ Rxf7 4. Qxf7 Nxe5 5. Rxe5 Qxe5 6. Qxd7 Qxc3 7. Rd1 Rf8, Black is up a healthy pawn and has every reason to hope for an eventual win. Yes, it takes a little work to figure out the line, but isn't that better than playing scared with 1. ... Ne7, which Black lost with? (Kurzdorfer-Don Christie, Buffalo, 1986).

♟ ♞ ♜ ♛

Don't be afraid of complications when going after something worthwhile. A good, sound position will not suffer from razzle-dazzle. But running scared will usually garner its just reward.

Principle 61: If you sacrifice material for the initiative, make sure that initiative is enduring, or at least that it can be exchanged for some gain elsewhere.

Many times it is not possible to calculate a sacrifice through to checkmate. They don't all work that well, for one thing. But you can make an intelligent decision as to whether the sacrifice is good to play by looking ahead a few moves and ascertaining whether you still have an initiative.

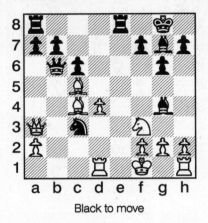

Black to move

Black seems to be in trouble. His queen and knight are in danger, and there is no way to hold on to both. But he takes advantage of the exposed White king to ensure a long-lasting initiative. This initiative had better last long; he begins the attack by giving up his queen! After 1. ... Be6 2. Bxb6 Bxc4+ 3. Kg1 Ne2+ 4. Kf1 Nxd4+ 5. Kg1 Ne2+ 6. Kf1 Nc3+ 7. Kg1 axb6 8. Qb4 Ra4 9. Qxb6 Nxd1, Black has a pawn, two bishops, and a rook for his queen, and he still has the initiative! (Robert Byrne-Bobby Fischer, New York, 1956).

Investing is a good thing only when you can be reasonably sure you will get some sort of return on your investment.

Principle 62: Accept a sacrifice not with the idea of holding on to the material, but with the idea of later gaining something by giving the material back.
World Champion Emanuel Lasker taught that we should accept the sacrifice of an important pawn any time we have a sound position, with the stipulation that we should be ready to give it up later rather than fall behind in development.

If you do not capture the pawn when it is offered, it may come back to haunt you later. If you hang on to your ill-gotten gains at the expense of developing your pieces, that policy may also come back to haunt you. So capture the offering, but allow your opponent (after exerting some time and effort) to gain it back later.

A good example of this principle is the Lasker Variation of the Evans Gambit, in which Black accepts the gambit pawn, but later plays to stifle White's attack, giving the pawn back in order to do so: 1. e4 e5 2. Nf3 Nc6 3. Bc4 Bc5 4. b4 Bxb4 5. c3 Ba5 6. 0-0 d6 7. d4.

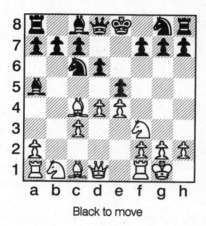

Black to move

7. ...Bb6 8. dxe5 dxe5 9. Qb3 Qf6 10. Bg5 Qg6 11. Bd5 Nge7 12. Bxe7 Kxe7 13. Bxc6 Qxc6 14. Nxe5 Qe6

Don't hang on for dear life to everything you have. Sometimes it is better to give something back in order to be in a better position later.

Principle 63: The only way to refute a gambit is to accept it.
This is a very practical piece of advice. Of course, some gambits are not refutable, so you have to be careful not to read into this principle too literally. It does not state "Accept all gambits." You have to decide whether the gambit is sound or unsound, and then play accordingly.

For instance, the Smith-Morra Gambit begins 1. e4 c5 2. d4 exd4 3. c3.

Black to move

If you don't believe that White should be able to give center pawns away like that, then accept the gambit and weather the attack with 3. ... dxc3. But if you are not interested in proving the gambit unsound and just want a playable game, you can always play 3. ... Nf6 or 3. ... d5. Just don't expect that you will be getting the better game.

Take the bull by the horns if you want to accomplish anything worthwhile. You won't get anywhere if you don't try. Star Wars' Yoda was wrong. There is "try." You just have to believe in your tries, and put all your effort into them.

Principle 64: A knight, firmly ensconced in a hole deep in the opponent's territory, is worth a rook.

Here is another very technical principle from Lasker. It is a good one to keep in mind when the opportunity arises to gain such an advantage, or when fighting against one.

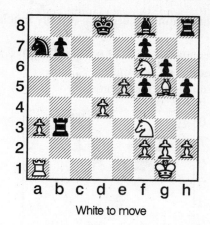

White to move

From the formula, it is clear that White is actually ahead in material (by a pawn), rather than down an Exchange for a pawn. After 1. e6, Black felt obliged to play 1. ... Rxf3 in order to prevent the other knight from arriving at e5 (another knight with the strength of a rook!), with the accompanying threats of 2. Nxf7+ and 2. Nxg6, picking up the h8-rook. After 2. Nd5+ Kc8 3. e7 Bg7, White finally took the rook with 4. gxf3, and had an actual material advantage, along with the powerful passed pawn on e7 (Kurzdorfer-Malcolm Mast, N Tonawanda, NY, 1986).

♟ ♞ ♜ ♛

Knowing the rationale behind why a rule has been made will allow you to adjust when circumstances are different. Therefore, if you give yourself a certain amount of time to get to the airport under normal conditions, you'll know to allow extra time if your flight is scheduled around the time of rush hour traffic or when security is particularly tight at the airport. The changed circumstances affect your scheduling.

Principle 65: **Three minor pieces are usually much stronger than a queen.**

This is another formula that is good to know. When you know you are getting three minor pieces for your queen, you aren't even sacrificing! Your opponent is doing the sacrificing.

White to move

In this theoretical position from the Queen's Gambit Declined, White does well to play 1. Nf4. What he must avoid is 1. Ne4, since Black gets a powerful position with the combination 1. ... Qxd5 2. Nf6+ gxf6 3. Bxd5 Bxd5.

♟ ♞ ♜ ♛

Even in his prime, Michael Jordan couldn't do it all alone. Remember to get help.

Chapter 14

Strategy

*"Tactics is what you do when you know what to do,
and strategy is what you do when you don't."*
—Siegbert Tarrasch

"First restrain, next blockade, lastly destroy!"
—Aron Nimzovich

Long-range ideas that help you achieve the result you want are called strategy. This includes any conceivable plan that can't be immediately implemented. Combinations and tactical moves are the means with which to carry out strategy.

Principle 66: Maintain the tension in the position rather than dissipating it too soon.
This principle applies to pawns staying put side-by-side rather than pushing one or exchanging one too soon. But it also applies to the position as a whole, particularly in the center.

The reason for maintaining tension is so that when you do break it, you can do so with explosive authority, making a difference in the position. You lose that chance by taking action too early.

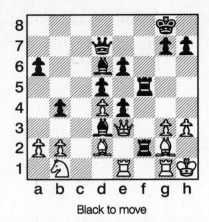

Black to move

In this famous position, Black doesn't do anything spectacular. His pieces are well placed, so he waits for White to make a weakening move (there's no other kind of move available to White!). In effect, Black forces his opponent to dissipate the tension, to his great discomfort with 1. ... h6.

There is nothing White can do. On 2. Nc3 bxc3; on 2. Bc1 Bxb1; on 2. Bf1 R5f3; on 2. Rd1 Re2; on 2. Rgf1 Bxf1; on 2. Kh2 R5f3; on 2. g4 R5f3 3. Bxf3 Rh2 mate (Fritz Saemisch-Aron Nimzovich, Copenhagen, 1923).

♟ ♞ ♜ ♛

> *"He who disturbs his position the least*
> *disturbs his opponent the most."*
>   —Old checker saying

Maintaining tension builds up over time. Your thoughts become more focused; carelessness is not allowed. Breaking this tension can easily rebound in favor of your opponent.

Think of watching a movie in a theater and on TV, where the tension is broken up by commercials. Which experience is more fulfilling?

Principle 67: The threat is greater than its execution.

Often it is better to leave a threat hanging over your opponent's head, like the sword of Damocles, than to carry it out. That way, your opponent has to constantly worry about the threat, which may well interfere with what she wants to do. After the threat is executed, a new situation occurs, and the old threat isn't a problem any more.

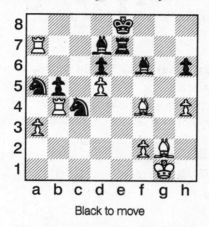

Black to move

In this complex setting, Black has two knights for rook and pawn. He can go after either rook with 1. ... Bc3 or 1. ... Bd4. But neither move works out too well: On 1. ... Bc3 White simply plays 2. Rb1 and nothing much has been accomplished. Even worse is 1. ... Bd4, in which White plays the surprising 2. Rxa5, since the bishop on d4 is not defended (that was the actual play in Kurzdorfer-GM Dmitri Gurevich, Washington, D.C., 1990).

But Black should let the threats hang over White's head with an in-between move, playing 1. ... Re1+. After 2. Kh2, the time is now ripe to carry out the now powerful move 2. ... Bc3, since the b4-rook has no safe escape.

Nimzovich was very sensitive to smoke. He was a very nervous person as well. Smoking was banned in the tournament room, but his opponent, Emanuel Lasker, took out a huge stogy, bit off the end, and placed it in his mouth. Nimzovich was very upset and immediately called the tournament director over, complaining about his opponent smoking. "But he isn't smoking," was the reasonable reply. "Ah," said Nimzovich, "but he is threatening to smoke, and you know that Herr Lasker is well aware that the threat is greater than its execution!"

♟ ♞ ♜ ♛

Don't carry out a threat until you are sure it can do the most damage.

Principle 68: Pawn majorities should be marched forward with the candidate leading.

This is another common-sense principle. Advancing a pawn that can be blocked by another pawn will likely stall your majority march.

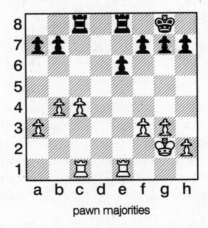

pawn majorities

Each side has a pawn majority. With White to move, the first player should start out with 1. c5, to be followed up with 2. b5 and 3. c6 if he wants to create a passed pawn. Beginning with 1. b5 meets with 1. ... b6, and Black's b-pawn holds back White's b- and c-pawns. No passed pawn is likely anymore.

Likewise, with Black to move, the second player should begin with 1. ... e5, followed by 2. ... f5 and 3. ... e4. Again, 1. ... f5 runs into 2. f4, and Black will not be able to create a passed pawn in the foreseeable future.

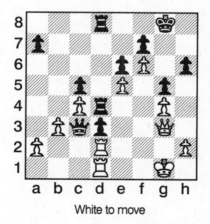

The candidate is the one that must step forward if she is to emerge victorious. Yes, she needs helpers, and lots of them, but the person trying to succeed must ultimately be the one to step forward in the clutch.

Principle 69: Attack the base of a pawn chain.

Pawn chains are only as good as their weakest link. Therefore, if you take out that link, the entire chain is destroyed.

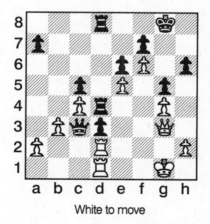

White to move

This is perhaps not the usual way to teach pawn chain strategy, but a pawn chain is a pawn chain. Here, White has two chains (a2-c4 and e5-f6) and Black has two chains (f7-e6 and h6-g5). White's chains are strong because there is no attack on either base (a2 or e5). Black, on the other hand, is vulnerable, since his chains defend his king and both bases are vulnerable. These considerations, along with the very important fact that the Black queen is out of play, outweigh Black's powerful passed d-pawn.

1. Qh3

White hits the base of one chain.

1. ... Kh7 2. Qh5

Now he hits the other base while keeping an eye on the first base.

2. ... R8d7 3. h4 Re4 4. hxg5

Now he hits a base yet again.

4. ... Qd4+ 5. Kh1, Black resigns (Kurzdorfer-Peretz Miller, Syracuse, NY, 1987).

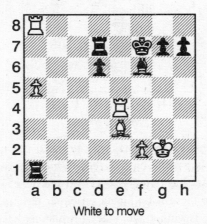

Take out the foundation and the entire structure collapses.

Principle 70: Rooks belong behind passed pawns.

The reason for this is simply that every time the pawn advances, the rook that is placed behind it increases in strength. Rooks placed in front of passed pawns actually lose strength as the pawn advances, while rooks placed at the side lose touch as soon as the pawn advances (but they get more mobility as a result).

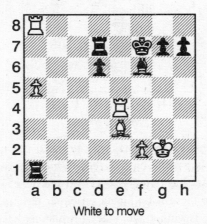

White to move

Each side has a passed pawn (we won't bother with the h-pawn, which isn't going anywhere any time soon). Black has both rooks placed behind passed pawns, while White's rooks are not in ideal positions. Therefore, Black has the better game, especially since he also has an extra pawn.

1. a6 d5 2. Rb4 d4 3. Rb7

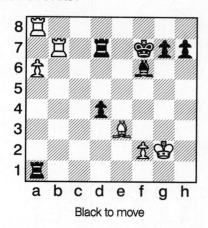

Black to move

It is White who has the threats, since his pawn is farther advanced. But Black should be all right after defending against the threat to e7 with 3. ... Re7 4. Bd2 Kg6.

The other side of the coin is that as a pawn advances, it too becomes stronger. Here that could cause trouble; White has several ways to go wrong. One is 3. ... Rxb7 4. axb7 and the pawn promotes. The other is 3. ... Ke7 4. Raa7, and the doubled rooks on the seventh rank combined with the advanced a-pawn win. This is what happened in the game (Barry Davis-Kurzdorfer, Buffalo, 1984).

The rook placed behind a passed pawn that gains squares every time the pawn moves is like a person with an open mind placed in a new situation where everything she learns increases her abilities. Traveling to a foreign country and learning the language will give anyone a broadened perspective. As we learn more and more, our horizons expand and we gain confidence.

Principle 71: **Blockade isolated, backward, and passed pawns, using a knight if possible.**

Passed pawns are a danger, so this principle makes a lot of sense with them. Isolated and backward pawns, on the other hand, are weak. They should be blockaded because otherwise they can advance, liquidating themselves in an effort to free up the pieces.

The reason a knight is the best blockader is twofold. First, it is the weakest piece, so it can be spared the job of keeping an eye on a pawn. Second, the peculiar hop of the knight is well suited to the task. A knight loses no mobility as a blockader. The next best blockader is the bishop. In endgames, where there is little danger of a quick mating attack, the king sometimes is an ideal blockader.

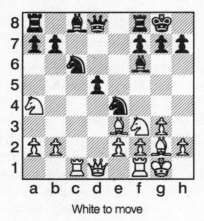

White to move

In this typical isolated d-pawn position White plays to blockade the isolated pawn, winding up with three blockaders and a solid advantage after 1. Nd4 Re8 2. Nc5 Nxd4 3. Bxd4 b6 4. Bxf6 Nxf6 5. Nb3 Bg4 6. f3 Bd7 7. Nd4.

Irritants of any kind need to be contained one way or another. Otherwise they get out of control.

Principle 72: Use a minority of pawns to attack a majority of pawns with the purpose of destroying the pawn structure of the majority.

It is generally better to attack when you have more pieces and pawns available. But sometimes you have the opportunity to attack three pawns with two or two pawns with one. That way, the pawn or pawns left over from the attack will be isolated or backward, and thus weak. Then you can go after the weakness with your pieces.

The Exchange Variation of the Queen's Gambit Declined often gives rise to this kind of minority attack.

A typical case begins 1. d4 Nf6 2. c4 e6 3. Nf3 d5 4. Nc3 Be7 5. cxd5 exd5 6. Bg5 c6 7. e3 Nbd7 8. Bd3 Nf8 9. Qc2 Ne6 10. Bh4 g6 11. 0-0 Ng7 12. Rab1 Bf5 13. b4 Bxd3 14. Qxd3 a6 15. a4 0-0.

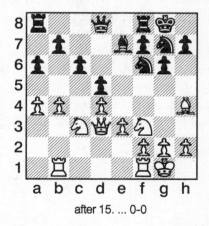

after 15. ... 0-0

It is clear that White is about to carry out the minority attack. The game continued 16. b5 axb5 17. axb5. If Black captures on b5, he will wind up with weak pawns on b7 and d5. So the play went 17. ...Ra3 18. Bxf6 Bxf6 19. Ra1 Qa5 20. Rxa3 Qxa3 21. bxc6 bxc6 22. Qc2 Nf5 23. Rb1 Nd6 24. Na4 Nc4 25. Nc5.

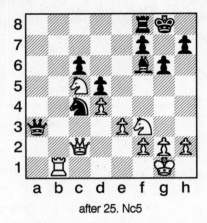

after 25. Nc5

Black has a weak, backward c-pawn that is solidly blockaded (David Hart-Kurzdorfer, San Diego, 1982).

♟ ♞ ♜ ♛

The short-handed goal in hockey is an example of a minority attack that most people are familiar with. A famous example from history is the battle of Marathon, where a relatively small number of Greeks successfully beat a large Persian army. A few knowledgeable, well-disciplined people can often overcome much larger numbers of adversaries.

Chapter 15

Defense

Defense is harder than attack, because it's more fun to attack and, psychologically, the burden of defense is often hard to bear. Also keep in mind, especially if you fancy yourself a defensive player, that there are very few good defenders in chess.

Principle 73: The best defense is a good attack.
This is an old truth that everybody involved in competitive sports and games has heard of. It is almost always true in chess. Examples of this principle are about as numerous as the number of chess games one can play. One will suffice:

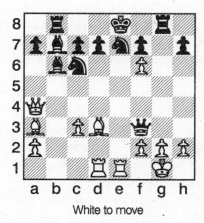

White to move

101

In the Evergreen Game, played in Berlin in 1851 between Adolph Anderssen and Jean Dufresne (one of the most famous games of all time), Black threatens checkmate. Defending g2 will not help in the least. The only way to avoid losing immediately is to throw a relentless attack at the Black king. That is just what Anderssen did. Behind by two knights to a pawn to begin with, he starts the final assault by giving up more material in order to get at the Black king:

    1. Rxe7+! Nxe7 2. Qxd7+!! Kxd7 3. Bf5+ Ke8 4. Bd7+ Kd8 5. Bxe7 mate.

Usually this principle does not show up in such a dramatic way, but it does show up frequently. Good players constantly attempt to impose their will on the position, defending against various threats by making stronger threats of their own.

♟ ♞ ♜ ♛

We know that if you want something to happen, you need to make it happen. And the way to make something happen is to go after it aggressively.

Principle 74: In Alekhine's Defense and other hypermodern openings, White has his initiative to defend.

This principle is the profound idea that a few masters had during and shortly after World War I. The hypermoderns freely gave their opponents a big, classical pawn center. Then they started chipping away at this center from the flanks. Alekhine's Defense (1. e4 Nf6 2. e5 Nd5), the Nimzo-Indian Defense (1. d4 Nf6 2. c4 e6 3. Nc3 Bb4) and the Reti Opening (1. Nf3 d5 2. c4) feature play of this kind, in which one player leaves her center pawns alone, setting up to attack the opponent's big pawn center from the flank.

A good illustration of this theme in action is this typical Gruenfeld Defense: 1. d4 Nf6 2. c4 g6 3. Nc3 d5 4. cxd5 Nxd5 5. e4 Nxc3 6. bxc3 Bg7 7. Bc4 0-0 8. Ne2 c5 9. Be3 Nc6 10. 0-0 Qc7 11. Rc1 Rd8 12. Qd2 Na5 13. Bd3 b6 14. f4.

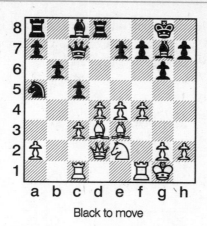

Black to move

Notice that Black has no pawns in the center, but he fights for the center squares all the same. The play continued 14. ... f5 15. Ng3 e6 16. e5 Bb7 17. Qf2 Rac8 and was eventually drawn (Clifton Kharroubi-Kurzdorfer, Buffalo, 1990).

♟ ♞ ♜ ♛

Boxers have the rope-a-dope. Backgammon players have the back game. Hypermodern chess is based on the idea that if you give your opponent enough rope, he might just hang himself.

Principle 75: Good attacking play wins games. Good defense wins championships.

It simply cannot be helped. Sometimes, no matter how hard you try to avoid it, you will have to go on the defensive in order to survive. So it is imperative that you have good defensive skills at your beck and call.

One skill you need is to first recognize that you must defend, and second recognize all the threats you must defend against. You must be aware that pawn moves should be kept to a minimum and that pieces need to come to your aid quickly. You have to know how to time your central counterattack and know when the time has come to give back your extra material, or even to give up some material in order to get a defensible position.

For a great defensive stand, it is hard to beat this:

White to move

In a world championship match, Black has sacrificed a pawn for a powerful attack. But White calmly repulses all the threats: 1. Qe2 Rad8 2. Rad1 Rxd1 3. Rxd1 h5 4. Nd6 Ba8 5. Bc4 h4 6. h3 Be3 7. Qg4 Qxe5 8. Qxh4 g5 9. Qg4 Bc5 10. Nb5 Kg7 11. Nd4 Rh8 12. Nf3 Bxf3 13. Qxf3 Bd6 14. Qc3 Qxc3 15. bxc3 Be5 16. Rd7 Kf6 17. Kg1 Bxc3 18. Be2 Be5 19. Kf1 Rc8 20. Bh5 Rc7 21. Rxc7 Bxc7 and the game was eventually drawn (Boris Spassky-Bobby Fischer, Reykjavik, Iceland, 1972).

In order to be a complete player—at any game—you must be well versed in all aspects of the game, including defense. Without good defense, you're just another attacking player. With it, you're a Player.

 Chapter 16

Calculation

"Genius is 99% perspiration and 1% inspiration."
—Thomas Edison

Combinations and plans have a better chance of working when they are backed up with good calculation. So how can you learn to find and accurately follow the various possibilities in front of you?

Principle 76: Look through the pieces' eyes.
Keep in mind that you are not actually playing the game—the pieces are playing. You're simply telling them where to go and when to go there. You are more of a coach than a player.

Therefore, it makes sense to let your pieces tell you where they want to go. They have a wonderful sense about these things, even if you don't. So listen to them. Learn to look at the position before you as the pieces look at it.

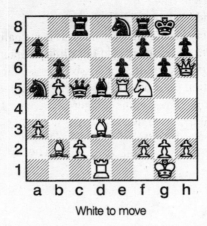

White to move

White has a bishop on b2, which leads directly to h8 and g7, a bishop on d3, which leads directly to g6 and h7, a rook on e5, which leads directly to h5 and a knight and queen already in the Black king's house at f5 and h6. Meanwhile, Black's king is surrounded by holes (e7, f6, h6) and more White pieces than Black. Do the White pieces want to find a way to get at the Black monarch? You bet they do!

The combination they want goes 1. Ne7+ Qxe7 2. Qxh7+ Kxh7 3. Rh5+ Kg8 4. Rh8 mate (Rudolf Spielman-Baldur Honlinger, 1929 match).

"Let it be."

—Paul McCartney

This is akin to the best teaching tradition: Facts are not poured into the student; rather, the teacher shows the student how to bring out what is already there.

Principle 77: Play blindfold games.

The hardest part of playing strong chess is calculating the various possible moves accurately: "If she goes here, I'll go there, then she will play the capture and I'll have to answer with . . ."

This can get very confusing in a hurry. It is virtually impossible to do with any amount of accuracy without diligent practice. One of the best ways to practice is to attempt to solve any diagram you come across without setting up a board and moving the pieces about. Also attempt to play entire games without sight of the board or pieces. This may prove impossible at first, but will come with practice.

The reason for these exercises is simply that you need practice following the play in your head without the physical crutch of seeing each and every position. You can't see these positions physically when you are calculating during a game after all, so that's what you need to practice.

In the following position, Harry Nelson Pillsbury was playing blindfolded, while simultaneously contesting fifteen other games, all without sight of the board!

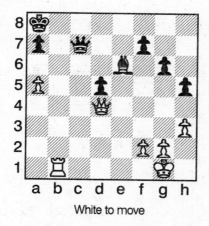

White to move

1. a6 Qc6 2. Qe5 Qc8 3. Qd6, Black resigns.
The threat of 4. Rb8+ Qxb8 5. Qc6+ is indefensible.

In order to make something that is intrinsically difficult easier, think about it and practice it a lot. Repetition will bring familiarity, and that will make anything seem easier.

Principle 78: Concentrate on forcing moves.

This is a hint that allows the most difficult calculations to become possible. There are perhaps somewhere in the vicinity of forty possible moves for each side in an average position. In order to look ahead at every possibility, then, you need to calculate your forty possibilities and each of your opponent's forty possible replies. That's 1,600 positions to assess and compare. All that for just ONE MOVE! Obviously, calculating six-move combinations (or even two-move combinations) in this way is impossible for humans to achieve.

But we don't really need to look at every possibility. Most of the possible moves do not follow any coherent plan and many are obviously downright bad. The key to checking multimove combinations is to concentrate on the forcing moves: checks, captures, promotions, and the immediate threats to check, capture, and promote. By cutting it down to these forcing moves, you now have some manageable numbers to work with. The moves you look at are the ones that will likely affect the outcome of the game.

White to move

I got this position in a correspondence game, so I had a chance to look far ahead, making sure the combination worked. The uncastled Black king on the same file as the queen-rook battery, with only a

White knight and a pinned Black bishop in the way, were the key ingredients that made me look for a winning combination. I could bypass looking at any move of the e7-bishop, since they all will be met with Nc6+, winning the Black queen.

1. Bg5 Rc7

The only other variation I really needed to check is the one beginning with the fork 1. ... f6. It is met with 2. Bxf6 gxf6 3. Qh5+ Ng6 4. Nxg6 hxg6 5. Qxh8+. Notice how each White move is either a check, a capture, or both.

2. Nxc5 Rxc5

The same answer awaits 2. ... f6 as before.

3. Nxf7 Kxf7 4. Bxe7 Qc8 5. Bxc5 Qxc5 6. Qe8+ Kf6 7. Qd8+ Kg6

The combination has ended with Black's king very exposed and his knight pinned, while White's rooks are ready to enter the attack.

♟ ♞ ♜ ♛

Looking at every possible variation is impossible and counterproductive in any endeavor. Concentrate on the essentials, and you will have a good chance of seeing your way through to a successful conclusion.

Principle 79: Never miss a chance to attempt to solve any position you come across.

The reason for this principle is simply that it is the best way to build up good habits. If you want your thinking to be disciplined when you are playing a game, then you must discipline your thinking even when you are not playing a game. That's how discipline works. It is not a sometime thing. It is ongoing.

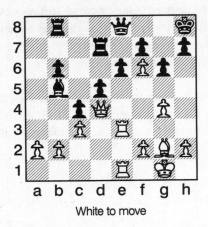

White to move

(Kurzdorfer-David Naiser, correspondence game, 1978). Did you figure it out? Time's up!

The solution is 1. Rxe6, when the rook cannot be taken because of the discovered check with 1. ... fxe6 2. f7+.

Build up good, sound habits daily. They will become a part of you, and when you find yourself in a critical position, you can hardly go wrong, because you won't know how!

Principle 80: Decide on your candidate moves and look at them each in turn.

This bit of advice comes from the wonderful book *Think Like a Grandmaster* by Alexander Kotov. In it, he explains how to go about calculating combinations that have a few variations. Jumping from one to the other and then back again will only muddle your brain. That is what most chess players probably do when looking ahead. But the strong player decides on the moves she will examine and then goes through each variation one at a time. She will then compare the positions at the end of each variation and decide which one she wants.

This may be hard to do at first. What if you miss a possible move among your original choices? Or what if you assess one or more of the resulting positions incorrectly? Or what if . . .? Of course you won't get everything right at first. You are not even likely to get everything right after years of study and practice. If chess were that easy, we wouldn't bother playing it.

But this method of thinking during a combination, or any variation, for that matter, gives you your best chance to see clearly into the position while staring at the position before you during a game.

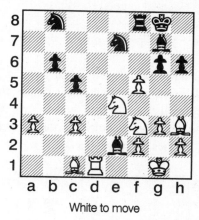

White to move

I got this position in a game after being surprised by a small combination that put my opponent's bishop on e2, forking my rook and knight. I saw the idea of f5-f6, getting the piece back, but didn't know how to also defend the e4-knight, so I played the interesting piece sacrifice 1. Rd6. But this was really unnecessary. I never considered the simpler 1. Re1, where White doesn't give up anything at all. The rook controls the e4-knight as well as the e7-knight from the e-file, so it should have been a candidate move (Kurzdorfer-Lesley Braun, Philadelphia, 1977).

♟ ♞ ♜ ♛

Know what your possibilities are before embarking on any endeavor.

Chapter 17

Piece and Pawn Cooperation

The relationships between pieces and pawns are intricate. Understanding these relationships is essential to good chess play.

Principle 81: Place your pawns on the opposite color square as your bishop.

This principle is usually acknowledged in the designation of good bishop versus bad bishop. Pawns capture diagonally forward, and bishops move diagonally. A good bishop is one placed well with respect to its pawns (on opposite-colored squares) while a bad bishop is placed badly with respect to its pawns (same-colored squares).

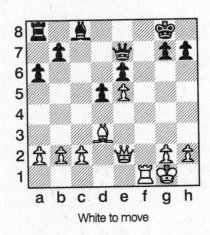

White to move

White's bishop has clear, open diagonals leading to both sides of the board. Black's bishop, on the other hand has one available square, after which it commands a diagonal that cannot hurt White. In addition, White has a lead in development. He wins by opening up the position with 1. Qh5 g6 2. Bxg6+ hxg6 3. Qxg6+, and Black's king is completely exposed to White's decisive attack.

♟ ♞ ♜ ♛

Unencumbered, free pieces are as happy as unencumbered, free people. Pieces in shackles are just as unhappy as people are in shackles.

Principle 82: Place your knight and pawns or your knight and bishop on the same-colored squares; that way they can control more squares.

This is the very same principle as the last one, only expressed a little differently, to accommodate the different individual pieces. Since knights always move to opposite-colored squares on the one hand, and bishops and pawns (when they capture) always move to same-colored squares, it is logical to place these different types of pieces on the same colored squares so they can work more efficiently together.

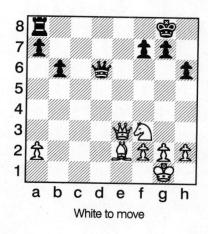

White to move

White has bishop and knight for rook and pawn. Furthermore, his bishop and knight are operating efficiently, since they are on the same-colored squares.

♟ ♞ ♜ ♛

Avoid duplication of effort for the most efficient results.

Principle 83: A good knight will overwhelm a bad bishop in an endgame even worse than a good bishop will.

A knight may be a bit slow in covering all the squares of a chessboard, but it will eventually get everywhere it wants. A bad bishop, on the other hand, isn't much use. Its own pawns get in the way, and it can only cover half of the squares on the board to begin with. This is not a fair match.

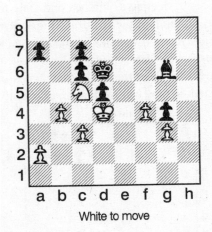

White to move

The knight towers over the bishop, and Black has no real chance any more as a result. The game concluded 1. a4 Bc2 2. a5 Bg6 3. a6 Bc2 4. Nb7+ Ke6 5. Kc5 Kd7 6. f5 d4 7. cxd4 Bxf5 8. Na5 Bd3 9. Nxc6 Bxa6 10. Nb8+, Black resigns (Curtis Hutchings, Jr.-Kurzdorfer, correspondence game, 1978).

Mobility is the key. The knight has it, while the bad bishop doesn't.

Principle 84: Possession of the bishop pair is often compensation enough for weak pawns.

The bishop pair covers all the squares on a chessboard much quicker than either a bishop and knight or two knights do. Therefore, the bishop pair is often an advantage, especially when the position is open and the bishops are controlling lots of squares.

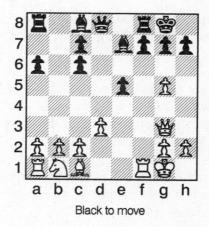

Black to move

Black's bishop pair will compensate for his poor queenside pawns if he can open the position, activating his pieces. The play went 1. ... e4 2. dxe4 Qd4+ 3. Qe3 Qc4 4. Qd3 Qxd3 5. cxd3 Rd8 6. Nc3 Be6 7. Bf4 Rxd3 8. Rad1 Rad8 9. Rxd3 Rxd3 10. Rf3 Rd7 11. h3 Bc4 12. Kh2 Bc5 13. Be3 Bd6+ 14. Bf4.

after 14. Bf4

Black can repeat the position with 14. ... Bc5 or try 14. ... Bxf4 15. Rxf4 Rd2, in which case his active rook now takes the place of the vanished bishop pair in compensating for the weak pawns (Walter Trice-Kurzdorfer, Worchester, MA, 1979).

♟ ♞ ♜ ♛

Weaknesses can be accepted as long as there is compensating strength. The trick is in knowing how much strength is necessary to offset any existing weakness.

Principle 85: A queen and knight complement each other and are often superior to a queen and bishop.

This principle is another manifestation of Principles 81 and 82. The queen and knight cover different squares, so there is no duplication. Therefore they work well together. The queen and bishop, on the other hand, often duplicate each other's efforts, and so are not as efficient working together.

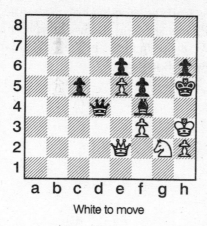

White to move

White is down a pawn and about to lose another pawn, but he has queen and knight to operate against the exposed Black king, and easily holds the draw: 1. Qb5 Bxe5 2. Qe8+ Kg5 3. Qe7+ Bf6 4. Qxe6 h5 5. f4+ Kh6 6. Ne3 Qc3 7. Kg2 Qb2+ 8. Kf3 Qb7+ 9. Ke2.

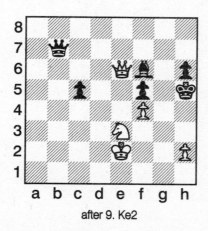

after 9. Ke2

The threats to f5 and f6 force Black to keep checking (Kurzdorfer-Hans Grupe, San Diego, 1982).

A good team is made up of individuals with different strengths—sometimes very different strengths. By using the best facets each team member has to offer, the team grows in strength, and the whole can be greater than the sum of its parts.

Chapter 18

Exchanges

You should know which pieces and pawns to exchange and when to exchange them. This is a very important aspect of chess strategy; don't neglect it.

Principle 86: Trade off your bad bishops.
In the French Defense, after 1. e4 e6 2. d4 d5 3. e5 b6 4. c3 Qd7 5. Nh3, Black, looking at the pawn chain f7-d5, decides to exchange his bad c8-bishop for White's good f1-bishop with 5. ... Ba6 6. Bxa6 Nxa6 7. 0-0 Ne7 8. Qe2 Nb8.

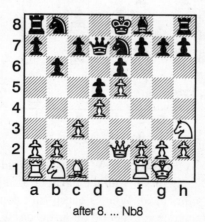

after 8. ... Nb8

Now White, looking at the pawn chain b2-e5, decides to return the favor, exchanging his own bad bishop on c1 for Black's good bishop on f8 with 9. b3 Nf5 10. Ba3 Bxa3 11. Nxa3 (Kurzdorfer-Peretz Miller, Syracuse, NY, 1987).

♟ ♞ ♜ ♛

Get rid of inefficiency and reward efficiency any way you can.

Principle 87: Trade your passive pieces for your opponent's active pieces.

This is an extension of Principle 86. The reason is obvious. Pieces that don't do much aren't as strong as pieces that do a lot. Therefore, if your bishop doesn't have much to do, while your opponent's bishop is an annoying piece, exchange them for each other if you can. If it's your knight that's bad and your opponent's knight that's good, trade them.

White to move

Black's queen is a royal pain. White can't avoid being harassed with 1. Bg2 Qh5+ 2. Kg1 Rg7, with the threat of 3. ... Nf4, nor with 1. Kh2 Qf4+. On the other hand, White's queen isn't doing much to help out. Therefore, the solution is to get rid of the queens with 1. Qg2, since after 1. ... Qxg2+ 2. Kxg2 Nf4+ 3. Kf3 Ne6 (Black can't win the bishop with 3. ... Nxh3 4. Rh1) 4. Rad1 White's king is safe and his pieces are well placed (Kurzdorfer-David Lavigne, New Hampshire, 1979).

If you had an opportunity to trade in an old, beat-up car for a newer, better model, you'd jump at the chance. Perhaps this sort of thing doesn't occur too often, but when it does we usually recognize the opportunity and quickly act on it. Usually, if it looks too good to be true, it is. But this sort of opportunity is not that rare in chess. In any case, always look to get the better of the bargain.

Principle 88: Trade your opponent's attacking pieces in order to break the attack.

This is simple common sense. If your opponent doesn't have any pieces, how can he continue the attack? Of course you must be careful not to leave the other guy with the few pieces that can do the most damage, and this isn't always so easy to avoid.

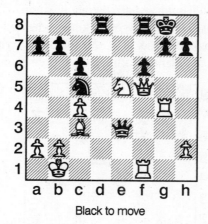

Black to move

White's attack looks ferocious. But by systematically eliminating most of the White pieces, Black comes out on top:

25. ... fxe5 26. Rxg7+ Kxg7 27. Bxe5+ Kh6

Definitely not 27. ... Kg8 28. Qg4+, when the attack is successful.

28. Bf4+ Qxf4 29. Qh3+ Kg5 30. Rxf4 Rxf4 and Black has two rooks and a knight for the only attacking piece White has left (Leonid Khinkis-Kurzdorfer, Buffalo, 1993).

In baseball, you can take the bat out of the hands of a home-run hitter by walking him. That has its dangers, of course, but at least he won't overwhelm you with a big blow. In tennis, you lob the ball over the head of an opponent rushing to smash the ball at the net. Taking a primary weapon away from an opponent is a great way to survive in any contest.

Principle 89: Trade pieces, particularly major pieces, when your pawn structure is healthier than your opponent's.

The reason for this principle is that as more and more pieces come off the board, the pawn structure becomes more and more important. Weak pawns suffer the most in endgames, and strong pawns are at their strongest in the endgame.

A good method is to visualize your position without pieces at every opportunity. That way, you'll know whether you should be playing for an attack, defense, or if you should be trying to exchange most of the pieces in order to reach a favorable endgame.

White to move

White has a healthy pawn majority on the kingside, while Black's pawn majority on the queenside is compromised. Therefore, White plays to exchange pieces, since the pure pawn ending is winning for him:

1. Qxg4

Of course 1. Qxe5 will get more pieces off the board—but at the cost of allowing opposite-colored bishops.

1. ... 0-0 2. f3 Rad8 3. Nd2 Ng6 4. Ne4 Qf5 5. Qxf5 Rxf5 6. Be3 Bd6 7. c4 c5 8. Rad1 h6 9. Rd2

White wants to trade on d6 only if he can keep Black's pawn structure compromised.

9. ... b6 10. Red1

Of course, winning a pawn will also make the endgame winning for White (Kurzdorfer-Robert Pill, correspondence game, 1980).

♟ ♞ ♜ ♛

Always keep the end goal in sight, no matter how complicated things may get in the meantime.

Principle 90: Exchange your opponent's blockading pieces in order to make room for passed pawns to march.

Since passed pawns have a lust to expand (Principle 30), it makes sense to give them room to do so. That's why the opponent wants to blockade the pawn (Principle 71) and that's why you want to break that blockade. One of the best ways to do so is to simply exchange the pieces that are doing the blockading.

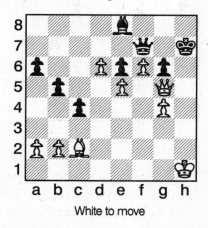

White to move

White has two passed pawns, and they want to march forward. But there are two Black pieces in the way. Therefore, White plays to remove those blockaders with 1. Qh5+ Kg8 2. Bxg6 Qxg6 3. Qxg6 Bxg6 4. d7, Black resigns (David Janowski-Simon Alapin, Barmen, Germany, 1905).

♟ ♞ ♜ ♛

Your path to success is clear after you remove obstacles that are in your way.

Principle 91: **Exchange your opponent's defending pieces in order to make room for your remaining attacking pieces to infiltrate.**

This may seem to contradict Principle 88, but it applies to different types of positions. The attacker needs to find a way to get on the opponent's home turf, and exchanging pieces is often a good way to do this. The key is naturally in knowing how many and which ones to exchange, while still leaving yourself enough pieces to finish the job.

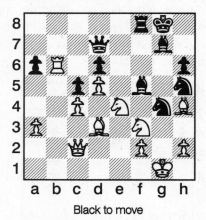

Black to move

Black is down a pawn and about to lose another pawn. But he has a substantial buildup of pieces in the vicinity of the White king, which lacks pawn protection.

1. ... Ne5 2. Nxe5 Bxe5 3. Rxa6 Bxe4 4. Bxe4 Qh3 5. Bg3 Nxg3
6. hxg3 Bd4

The attack is unstoppable (Fidelity B-Kurzdorfer, Philadelphia,
1988).

♟ ♞ ♜ ♛

When a clear path is necessary to achieve success, the astute individual will clear the path by any means necessary.

Chapter 19

Planning

*"It is not a move, even the best move,
that you must seek, but a realizable plan."*
—Eugene Znosko-Barovsky

*"Methodical thinking is of more use in
chess than inspiration."*
—C. J. S. Purdy

*"Whoever sees no other aim in the game than that of
giving checkmate to one's opponent will never become
a good chess player."*
—Max Euwe

Predicting the future is not easy, especially when you have an opponent who wants a different outcome. One good way to find a plan is to visualize the position without the pieces. Take into consideration only the pawn structure. Another good way is to picture any goal in your mind and find out a way to achieve it. This trick of visualizing an end result is a big help in formulating plans, and also in sticking to the plans you have come up with.

Principle 92: A bad plan is better than no plan at all.
About the worst thing you can do during a chess game is to make a move or, worse yet, a series of moves, with no guiding purpose. Your moves should have a relationship with each other, and should be based on the requirements of the given position.

A plan implies that there will be certain steps to take for obtaining a goal. This goal will usually be a subgoal to the overall plan of winning, or not losing, the game. Such large overall strategies are essential, but can only be carried out through a series of smaller, shorter-term plans. Grab control of more squares, disrupt your opponent's piece coordination or pawn structure, bring more pieces into play, or stake out your share of the center are a few examples of what you can do within a few moves.

Strive to gain something with each move or each series of moves, always making sure these moves fit together. Don't try to achieve unrelated goals from move to move or your game will quickly fall apart.

♟ ♞ ♜ ♛

Very little can be accomplished without an overall plan and numerous related steps to accomplish the goal. A project backed up with a second-rate plan is bound to produce better results than a project with no plan at all, since very little can be accomplished without an overall plan.

Principle 93: A good plan incorporates many little plans.
Of course your plan is to checkmate your opponent, or at least to prevent your own king from being checkmated. But that's too broad of a plan for the early stages of a game. You have to break up this overall plan into stages. First, you try for an opening advantage of some sort, or at least play to deny your opponent an opening advantage. Then, you move on to specific features of the position and focus on those. Each stage of the game will likely bring formidable obstacles in the form of your opponent's plans. So you concentrate on overcoming those obstacles while forwarding your plan. Simple, right?

Well, no. The idea is indeed simple, but carrying out these constantly shifting plans while attempting to keep everything under control is a complex process. But this is part of what attracts us to chess in the first place.

White to move

White has three pawns for a knight, and conceives of the plan of pushing the kingside pawns up together as far as they can go.

1. Be3

The alternative 1. Bg3 doesn't fit in with the plan, since it blocks the g-pawn.

1. ... Rad8

Black looks for counterplay in the center.

2. f4 Kg8 3. Rf1 h5

Now Black slows up the pawn advance.

4. g3

The move 4. h3 destroys White's whole plan after 4. ... h4.

4. ... g6 5. h3 Rd3 6. Kg2 b5 7. g4 a5

Black is now countering White's plan with a minority attack.

8. f5 gxf5 9. gxf5

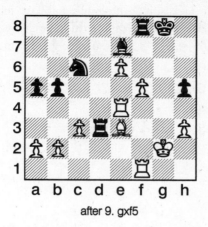

after 9. gxf5

White's plan has been carried out. Now it is time to make a new plan: Get the f-pawn to f6. Black naturally plays to blockade the pawn and the beat goes on (Kurzdorfer-IM Ed Formanek, Buffalo, 1992).

♙ ♞ ♜ ♛

Completing a huge task becomes possible when it is broken up into many connected little tasks. In other words, a journey of a thousand miles is carried out one mile at a time.

Principle 94: In isolated d-pawn positions, the plans are clearly spelled out.

There are many opening variations that lead to an isolated d-pawn position. In some of them White has the isolated pawn, in others it is Black who takes on the burden. One reason these positions are so popular is probably that the plans for each side are so clear.

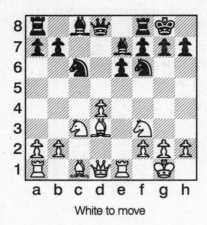

White to move

In this very typical isolated d-pawn position, White is the one with the isolated pawn. That means he has a weakness (the pawn cannot count on pawn support) as well as a strength (the pawn is in the center and controls important central squares).

White's plan is to develop his forces to good, aggressive squares, taking advantage of his greater spatial control and mobility. He will likely try to push the d-pawn if an opportunity arrives, or liquidate it, in either case increasing his mobility and spatial control.

Black will want to firmly blockade the pawn right where it is in order to hamper White's activity. She will thus try to plant a knight on d5 and defend against any attacks White can come up with. If Black can beat off the attack and exchange some of the pieces, she will have an endgame advantage.

White usually starts out with 1. a3, to prevent the maneuver ... Nb4-d5. This makes it more difficult for Black to carry out her plan.

In many positions the plans are not quite so clear as they are here. Nevertheless, in most cases you will do well to start with the pawn structure in order to determine which plans to attempt.

♟ ♞ ♜ ♛

Determine what is actually going on before coming up with a

plan of any kind. Tailor your plan according to the specific needs of the situation.

Principle 95: Keep your plans flexible.

Be ready for anything your opponent may throw your way. Your opponent will try to foil your plans. This means that plans that are flexible have the most chance of succeeding.

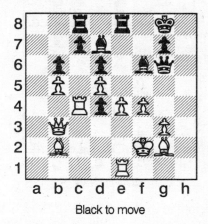

Black to move

In this complex position, Black defended his weak d-pawn by first counterattacking White's weak b-pawn, then attacking on the kingside, then using the a-file to activate the c8-rook and once again pressure the b-pawn. He then forced a queen trade to stop White's kingside attack before it started, then finally defended the pawn directly. The play went 1. ... d3 2. Bxf6 Qxf6 3. Rb4 g5 4. Ke3 gxf4+ 5. gxf4 Rf8 6. Rf1 Qh4 7. Qd1 Ra8 8. Rb3 Ra5 9. Qf3 Bg4 10. Qf2 Qxf2+ 11. Rxf2 Be2 (Joel Johnson-Kurzdorfer, Lowell, MA, 1979).

Centralized, mobile, well-developed pieces along with a healthy pawn structure made this kind of flexibility possible.

♟ ♞ ♜ ♛

The more options you have, the more likely your choices will be good ones.

Principle 96: In pawn chain, opposite-side castling positions, attack where your pawn chain is pointing.

This is a good rule of thumb no matter where your king resides. When the center is closed off in linked pawn chains, the attack is aimed at exploiting your strength and your opponent's weakness.

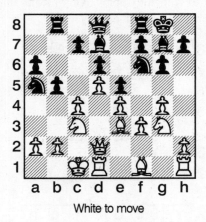

White to move

White will attempt to expose the base of Black's pawn chain, and that is c7. Thus a kingside attack will not get the job done. The play will more than likely go 1. c5 b4 2. c6 bxc3 3. Qxc3 Nxc6 4. dxc6 Be6 then 1. h4 with the idea of 2. h5 and 3. hxg6 fxg6, which will only open the f-file for Black's rook to harass White's pawn chain base at f3.

♟ ♞ ♜ ♛

Keep the big picture in mind when deciding what action to initiate. Often it is better to attempt to exploit your special strengths than to go for an immediate haymaker, which can easily backfire.

Chapter 20

Openings

Sometimes, the game will start out with a bang. Other times it may start out with a yawn. How much do you know about your opening?

Principle 97:

> *"Your only task of the opening is*
> *to get a playable middlegame."*
> —GM Lajos Portisch, from *How to Open a Chess Game*

This is a practical bit of advice in direct contrast with the generally accepted opening theory that White should try for an advantage, while Black should play to equalize. The trouble with this theory is that in order to seriously attempt to play for an opening advantage, White has to know an impossible amount of theory. For anybody who is not a chess professional, it is better to simply try for a playable position— preferably one the player is familiar with.

A good way to get a playable game is to play less well known, but sound openings. A good example is the Exchange Variation of the Ruy Lopez (1. e4 e5 2. Nf3 Nc6 3. Bb5 a6 4. Bxc6) and another is the King's Indian Attack (begin with 1. Nf3, 2. g3, 3. Bg2, 4. 0-0). For Black you might try the Scandinavian Defense (1. e4 d5 2. exd5 Qxd5 3. Nc3 Qa5) or the Queen's Gambit Accepted (1. d4 d5 2. c4 dxc4).

With these choices you are not trying to blow your opponent off the board. You are just trying to stay alive, aiming for a type of middlegame position you are familiar with.

Don't try to grab everything all at once. Ambition is good, but it has to be based on something. Over ambition is self-defeating. Get off to a good start each day, and take it from there. Build up your resources before attempting to cash in.

Principle 98:

> *"When caught in an opening you don't know, play healthy, developing moves."*
> —GM Bent Larsen from *How to Open a Chess Game*

This is a wonderful bit of advice from someone who knows (Larsen was famous for experimenting in the openings). Wild piece sacrifices, tricky maneuvers, and excessive pawn moves are not healthy if you don't know every specific in detail. So stick with the tried and true central development. You won't go too far wrong.

Eric Schiller-Kurzdorfer, Bradford, PA, 1992 began 1. d4 Nf6 2. Nf3 g6 3. Bg5.

This was the first time I had to meet this move in this position.

3. ... Ne4

Is this a healthy developing move? Well, it does threaten to misplace White's knight while gaining the bishop pair, and it does place the knight in the center. I knew the move was supposed to be good.

4. Bh4 Bg7 5. Nbd2 d5 6. e3 c5

Pressuring the center and making room for the queen can be considered healthy development.

7. c3 Nc6 8. Bd3

White begins making threats.

8. ... cxd4 9. exd4 Bf5 10. Qe2

How can Black defend against the threat to e4 while completing development? It can be done with a few well-timed exchanges.

10. ... Nxd2 11. Qxd2 Bxd3 12. Qxd3 Qd7

White's pin along the d8-h4 diagonal has finally been broken.

13. 0-0 0-0

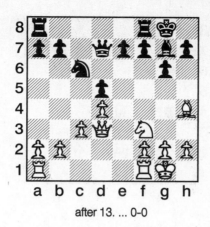

after 13. ... 0-0

Development has been successfully completed.

♟ ♞ ♜ ♛

The tried-and-true is true for a reason. Stick with it, unless there is a very good reason not to.

Principle 99: In open games, get the pieces developed and the king safe, and do it quickly.

This is so important. If you do not get developed quickly and get the king out of the middle in open games, you will regret it. The following is one example out of thousands (Aron Nimzovich-Simon Alapin, Riga, Latvia, 1913): 1. e4 e6 2. d4 d5 3. Nc3 Nf6 4. exd5 Nxd5 5. Nf3 c5 6. Nxd5 Qxd5 7. Be3 cxd4 8. Nxd4 a6 9. Be2 Qxg2 10. Bf3 Qg6 11. Qd2 e5 12. 0-0-0 exd4 13. Bxd4 Nc6.

after 13. ... Nc6

White first sacrificed a pawn, then a piece, in an effort to keep Black undeveloped and his king in the middle. He has succeeded beautifully. Now he uncorks a scintillating combination that finished the game in a hurry.

14. Bf6 Qxf6 15. Rhe1+ Be7

No better is 15. ... Be6 16. Qd7 mate.

16. Bxc6+ Kf8

Or 16. ... bxc6 17. Qd8 mate.

17. Qd8+ Bxd8 18. Re8 mate.

This sort of thing happens every day to unwary players who sluggishly go about their development in an open game.

♟ ♞ ♜ ♛

Falling behind can have disastrous consequences when there is a tight deadline. Don't let it happen to you!

Principle 100: In queen pawn games, do not obstruct the c-pawn.
This is simply because the c-pawn can help as an attacker or a defender of some very important central squares. Also, moving the c-pawn gives your queen some room to roam.

The similar case of the f-pawn in king pawn games is complicated by the presence of the king. Moving the f-pawn in those positions can expose his majesty, and that is not advisable.

One of the normal move orders in the Queen's Gambit Declined illustrates this principle very well: 1. d4 d5 2. c4.

This is considered superior to 2. Nc3, which develops a piece to a good square but shuts in the c-pawn.

2. ... e6 3. Nc3 Nf6 4. Bg5 Nbd7

And not 4. ... Nc6, which places the knight on a better square but blocks the c-pawn.

5. Nf3 c6

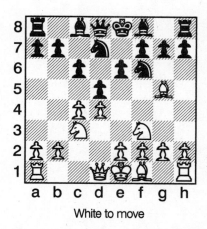

White to move

White has used his c-pawn for attack, while Black has used her c-pawn for defense.

Paying attention to small details can often mean the difference between success and failure.

Principle 101: As Black, play to equalize.

Until you have equalized, it's not a good idea to look for a way to gain an advantage. Too many players get impatient with Black and try to wrest the initiative without first equalizing. Infamous semisound openings that attempt to punish White for playing perfectly good, sound moves are the Latvian Gambit (1. e4 e5 2. Nf3 f5) and the Albin Counter Gambit (1. d4 d5 2. c4 e5).

It's much better to play healthy developing moves (Principle 98), aiming to equalize in the center.

♟ ♞ ♜ ♛

When you're behind to begin with, it's better to catch up before you forge ahead.

Chapter 21

Middlegames

"Before the endgame, the gods have placed the middlegame."
—Siegbert Tarrasch

After the pieces have come into the action and the kings are settled in, the middlegame takes over.

Principle 102: The transition to the middlegame will often require a lot of thought.

Transition phases are always difficult, since there are so many choices that can mark the character of the game for a long time to come. The important idea behind this principle is to recognize such phases when they occur, so you can take the necessary time to formulate a plan.

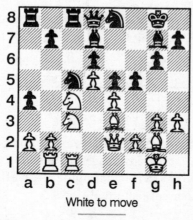

White to move

White has a central space advantage out of a King's Indian Defense, but will find himself behind the eight ball in a hurry if he doesn't do something aggressive right now, since Black is threatening to smother the queenside with 1. ... b5 2. Nd2 b4. Meanwhile, White has most of his pieces posted around the queenside, so he should reasonably expect an advantage there.

White conceives of the idea of driving out the Black c5-knight in order to get a White knight to b6. He uses pawn moves in order to carry out this plan, which has the bonus point of opening up files for his rooks. The play went:

1. b4 axb3 e.p. 2. axb3 b5 3. Nb6

This is a case of a tactical resource aiding the strategic idea.

3. ... Qxb6 4. b4 Qa6 5. bxc5 dxc5 6. Nxb5 Nd6 7. Nc3 Qxe2 8. Nxe2 c4 9. Nc3

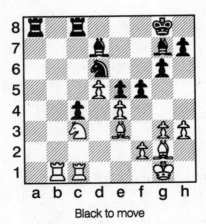

Black to move

The transition into the middlegame is complete. White has retained his central space advantage while taking control of many open queenside lines with his suddenly well-placed pieces (Kurzdorfer-Greg Henry, Bradford, PA, 1990).

Unlike in the subatomic world, life is rarely made up of discrete quantified bursts of energy. Neither is chess. The game flows from beginning to end, as does life, and we must help that flow out by recognizing transition times and acting on them accordingly.

Principle 103: Look to the pawn structure in order to come up with a plan.

This is simply because the pawn cannot ever retrace its steps. Therefore, pawns generally tend to remain where they are for a long time. When they do move, weak squares are produced in their wake.

When coming up with a plan, keep this property of pawns in mind. It is the key to most successful plans.

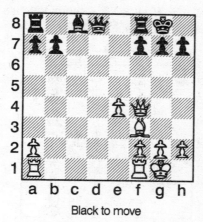

Black to move

White has a pawn majority in the center and more pieces on the kingside. Black has a pawn majority on the queenside and also more pieces on the queenside to back up the majority. Therefore, Black marches his pawns on the queenside while White attempts to advance in the center and attack on the kingside. The play went:

1. ... b5 2. Rfd1 Qe7 3. Rac1

Black changes his plan. He now will play on the open c-file, even though the pawn structure does not demand that he do so. He might try 3. h4 for the kingside attack or 3. Rab1 to menace Black's pawn majority.

3. ... Be6 4. Rc7 Qa3 5. e5 Rac8 6. Rdc1 Rxc7 7. Rxc7 Qxa2

Black has won a pawn, and his passed pawns proved to be quicker than the White kingside attack (Thomas Thrush-Kurzdorfer, correspondence game, 1990).

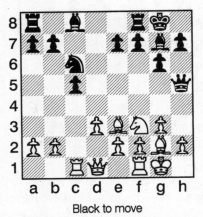

By taking the least mobile units into account when formulating your plan, you come up with a plan that has great chances of succeeding.

Principle 104: Make sure all your pieces are defended.

Leaving one or more of your pieces without defense sets you up for surprise tactical assaults. If all the pieces are defended to begin with, you will have little to fear.

Black to move

Black notes that his c-pawn is under fire from rook and bishop. He can exchange it for White's b-pawn with 1. ... Bxb2 2. Rxc5, but then his bishop is vulnerable and his queen is under attack. Or he can simply block the bishop's diagonal with 1. ... Nd4.

What he must avoid is the innocent-looking pawn defense 1. ... b6, since that move leaves knight and rook vulnerable to the shot 2. Ng5 Bd7 3. Bf3 Qh6 4. Ne6, snaring an Exchange.

If you don't want your weaknesses exploited, eliminate them.

Principle 105: Build up small advantages when a combination is not available.

This is another common sense guideline that gives you an idea of how to go about trying to win a game when your position is not yet winning. Let's face it, that's most of the time.

There is often no rush when going about the business of winning a game. Usually advantages have to be accumulated, while making sure that counterplay does not develop. This is something that takes constant vigilance.

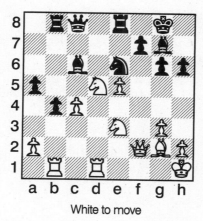

White to move

White has a big space advantage in the center, but this is not enough by itself to win. So he first aims at the weak f6-square, then takes over the f-file:

1. Ng4 Kf8 2. Ngf6 Rd8 3. Rf1 Rb7

Next comes a reposition of the king (to make him safer) and b1-rook (to the more open d-file).

4. Kg1 h5 5. Rbd1 Bh6

Finally, White is ready to penetrate into the weak Black position with the winning breakthrough:

after 5. ... Bh6

6. Nb6 Qc7 7. Nfd7+ Kg8 8. Qxf7+ Kh8 9. Qxe6 (Kurzdorfer-Andrew Karklins, Buffalo, 1994).

Don't let up for a second. Constant striving is one of the big keys to victory.

Chapter 22

Endings

"Pawn endings are to chess what putting is to golf."
—C. J. S. Purdy

The endgame is not necessarily the end of the game. Rather, it is that part of the game when few pieces are left, and the kings and pawns take on a greater role than they had in earlier phases of the game.

Principle 106: The king is a fighting piece—use it!
When there is little or no danger of a checkmating attack (like there constantly is in most openings and middlegames), you might as well use what few resources you have left and boldly bring your king into the attack.

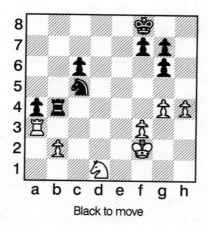

Black to move

Black has an extra pawn, but his rook and knight are doing all they can. It's time for the king to enter into the fray to mop up:

36. ... Ke7 37. Ke3 Kd6 38. Ra2 Ke5 39. Nc3 Rd4 40. Ra3 Rd3+ 41. Kf2 Kd4 42. Ke2 Re3+ 43. Kf2 Nd3+, White resigns. (Jim Huston-Kurzdorfer, correspondence game, 1993)

Throw everything at 'em, including the kitchen sink. There's no need to hold back when the danger is past.

Principle 107: The aim of most endgames is to promote a pawn.
Checkmate is the aim of all chess games. But late in the game, when most of the pieces are no longer on the board, checkmate is rarely possible. This is the time to find a way to promote a pawn. With an extra queen, most players, regardless of their strength, will find a way to checkmate.

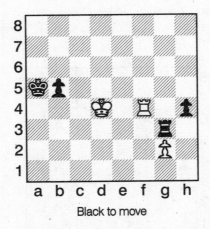

Black to move

Black is not interested in counting pawns or in trying to devise a mating attack. The only thing that matters is to get that passed pawn to b1:

1. ... b4 2. Rxh4 b3 3. Rh5+ Kb4 4. Rh8 b2 5. Rb8+ Ka3 6. Ra8+ Kb3 7. Rb8+ Ka2 8. Ra8+ Ra3, White resigns (James Walker-Kurzdorfer, Mansfield, OH, 1993).

Most workers revel in a chance at promotion. We do what we can to earn promotions, and try hard to show that we are worthy. Seize any chance to step up the ladder.

Principle 108: Make use of Zugzwang, triangulation, and coordinate squares in endgames.

Good players are always on the lookout for these subtle endgame strategies. Zugzwang is the compulsion to move, triangulation is a way to put the opponent in Zugzwang, and coordinate squares are the ones you try to control when triangulating.

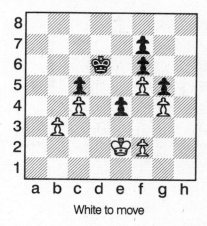

White to move

The coordinate squares are e3 and e5. Any time the White king arrives at e3, Black had better be ready to answer by moving her king to e5 in order to save the e4-pawn. Since going to e3 directly runs into 1. Ke3 Ke5, White uses the triangulating maneuver, using the route e2-d2-e3:

    1. Kd2 Ke5 2. Ke3

Black must give way now; she is in Zugzwang (Nedelkovich study).

Use all the tools of your trade. Even rarely used, specialized knowledge will come in handy from time to time. Don't forget any basic knowledge, no matter how esoteric it may appear to be.

Principle 109: A crippled pawn majority will have difficulties creating a passed pawn.

This is because the candidate pawn is taken off the open file, where it is needed in order to become a passer. The Exchange Variation of the Ruy Lopez is an opening played with the idea of crippling Black's queenside pawn majority (1. e4 e5 2. Nf3 Nc6 3. Bb5 a6 4. Bxc6 dxc6).

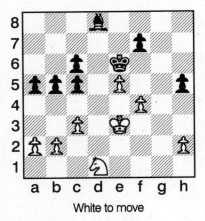

White to move

This is the kind of position White is trying for in this variation. White will be able to form a passed pawn with his central majority by preparing to march the pawns and then marching them. Black will not be able to form a passed pawn at all without help from White. From the figure, the play went:

1. c4 Kf5 2. Kf3 Ke6 3. Nc3 f6 4. Ke4 fxe5 5. f5+ Kf6 6. cxb5 cxb5 7. Nxb5 Bb6 8. Nc3 Ba7 9. h4 c4 10. Nd5+ Kf7 11. Kxe5

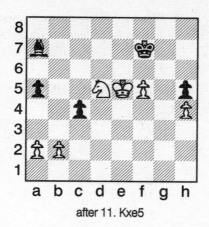

after 11. Kxe5

White has an extra passed pawn. Black has nothing but weak pawns.

Handicaps are hard to overcome. Don't saddle yourself with any if you can help it.

Principle 110: When in doubt, do anything but push a pawn.

One of the sayings you sometimes hear among amateur players is "When in doubt, push a pawn." This is one of the worst pieces of advice on playing chess that I have ever heard. Every time a pawn moves, it leaves weakened squares in its wake. Therefore, this is the one thing you do not want to do unless you have a very good reason for the push.

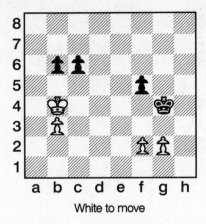

White to move

King moves keep the game level. Pawn moves lose. This is the type of situation to keep in mind at all times during a chess game, because the consequences of a hasty or ill-considered pawn move so often lead to disaster, like here.

♟ ♞ ♜ ♛

Be extra careful when making a decision that cannot be reversed.

Part II
Human Matters

"The world is not likely to tire of an amusement which never repeats itself, of a game which presents today features as novel and charms as fresh as those with which it delighted, in the morning of history, the dwellers on the banks of the Ganges and the Indus."

—Willard Fiske

"Chess holds its master in its own bonds—fetters and in some ways shapes his spirit, so that under it the inner freedom of the very strongest must suffer."

—Albert Einstein

The one area in which humans still completely baffle the electronic monsters (computers) is just that area where the special genius of the Homo sapien shines: It is intuition and the ability to grasp the greater picture. This is Tao at its best, and nobody yet has been able to program silicon chips to seek truth the way humans can.

Part II deals with the more human principles of life and chess. These principles come to light in any competitive mind game, but are particularly relevant in the game of chess.

Chapter 23

Know Yourself

"The way he plays chess demonstrates a man's whole nature."
—Stanley Ellin

"You cannot play at chess if you are kind-hearted."
—French proverb

Knowing yourself includes knowing your style, proclivities, will to win, capacity for hard work, and so many other bits of information about yourself. If you do not know these things about yourself, you are probably your own worst enemy during a chess game.

A strong opponent will learn things about you during a game that you didn't know. For instance, if you are careless in your opening research but work very hard during a game searching for tactical play that makes the most of your chances, players will soon learn this and get you into positions where tactics are not likely to crop up. Perhaps you could work a little harder to find a way to force the types of positions you excel at.

Since this is a good piece of advice in whatever you may get involved in, why not take the time and effort to find out just who you are during a chess game? The knowledge will pay off in so many ways.

Principle 111: Style can be more important than strength.
This one may not seem intuitive, but it is often true. Here's a scenario

familiar to so many chess players, especially those who play the same people often: Player A regularly defeats Player B, who regularly handles Player C, who in turn regularly trounces Player A. Obviously mere strength of play is not enough to explain such results. But style and personality can indeed explain these triangles.

One of my triangles involved two other national chess masters from Buffalo, New York. Bem Tyehimba was usually rated well above Lionel Davis and me. Bem was the strongest of the three, and it was no surprise that he regularly took care of Lionel, defeating him in a match and almost always whenever they met. Bem had a very calm, steady style. He would lay in wait for his opponents to try to attack him, and turn back those attacks with precise technique. Lionel was just the opposite. He would go after you, no matter what your strength. He loved to cause trouble for opponents, making one threat after another. Lionel's style played right into Bem's hands.

But that same devil-may-care attitude that Bem handled so easily gave me fits. I had terrible trouble trying to hold back Lionel whenever we played, and usually wound up on the losing end of our encounters.

Bem, on the other hand, notwithstanding his strength, gave me no trouble at all. I played very patiently, slowly building up my position, never attacking until I had a real advantage. Though he was a stronger player, I won most of our games, regardless of whether I had the White or Black pieces.

♟ ♞ ♜ ♛

Be aware of your style and your opponent's style. It is, after all, very much part of who you both are.

Principle 112: Strive to get into positions you are comfortable with.

Once you know what your likes and dislikes are, you can decide which types of positions you enjoy handling the best. Those are the ones to strive for, whether or not they are considered best by theory.

Do you like open positions where the pieces can fly about at will? Then play the Queen's Gambit Accepted or the Open Ruy Lopez, but stay away from defenses like the Closed Ruy Lopez or King's Indian Defense. Like maneuvering behind closed lines and pawn chain games where strategy is usually more important than tactics? Then play the French and Nimzo-Indian Defenses, but stay away from the open gambits.

♟ ♞ ♜ ♛

When you are comfortable with whatever you are doing, you will probably do it well.

Principle 113: Know your limitations.

If you cannot see past more than three or four moves, it makes little sense to attempt a twenty-move combination involving great material sacrifice that must be precisely calculated. It doesn't matter if the combination might win. You'll be better off trying something a little more modest.

Likewise, if you have trouble memorizing long opening lines, you should stay away from popular openings such as the Dragon Sicilian (1. e4 c5 2. Nf3 d6 3. d4 cxd4 4. Nxd4 Nf6 5. Nc3 g6), in which the main lines go well past Move 20, or obscure but highly tactical sacrificial attacks such as the Wilkes-Barre (1. e4 e5 2. Nf3 Nc6 3. Bc4 Nf6 4. Ng5 Bc5). It's better to play healthy developing moves (Principle 98), and stay within your limitations.

♟ ♞ ♜ ♛

Sports people often talk about "playing within yourself." But this is something that applies to people in all walks of life. It simply means don't strive for more than you are capable of.

Principle 114: Know your strengths.

Are you a good defender? (There aren't many.) If you are one of the exceptions, then play solid openings in which you will have a chance to do what you do best. Are you good at calculating long variations?

Then play for those wild complications.

Your greatest strength is not necessarily what you enjoy most about the game. Your greatest strength is what gives you the best results. For instance, when looking through master games, I always admired players like Mikhail Tal and Alexei Shirov. Their exciting sacrificial combinations are always a great source of inspiration. But I can't play like that very often, at least not very successfully. I'm usually at my best when patiently maneuvering—accumulating small advantages. It's just that such a style of play isn't very attractive. But it does bring in many wins.

♟ ♞ ♜ ♛

Stick with what you do best and your results will be as good as they can be.

Principle 115: Choose the competitions best suited to you.

Do you like speed chess? Then Rapid tournaments (with a time limit of Game in thirty minutes or fewer) and possibly Internet chess will appeal to you. You'd probably also like five-minute chess or three-minute chess, or whatever variant of blitz is played in your neighborhood. But if speed chess stresses you out because you have trouble making fast decisions, then perhaps it is best to stay away from those types of competitions.

If you like to take your time figuring out what is going on during a game, and feel you need long periods of thinking time to calculate variations and devise strategy, then play in the slower time-limit tournaments, or even get into correspondence play.

If you prefer casual play, stay away from tournaments. If you prefer structure, stay away from skittles.

♟ ♞ ♜ ♛

When you play under conditions you enjoy, you're already a winner.

Chapter 24

Know Your Opponent

*"Could we look into the head of a chess player,
we should see there a whole world of feelings, images,
ideas, emotion, and passion."*

—Alfred Binet

*"A man that will take back a move at chess
will pick a pocket."*

—Fenton

You don't play chess in a vacuum. Your opponent is trying to thwart everything you do. It is a very good idea in any competition to know what you are up against.

Principle 116: Strive for positions that make your opponent uncomfortable.

This is much easier to do if you know your opponent well. But what if you know nothing whatsoever about him or her? Then you must find clues in playing style and body language.

When your opponent is uncomfortable, that gives you an edge. The great master of this style of play was Emanuel Lasker, whose opponents could never figure out what he was going to do next.

For instance, in a must-win game, Lasker played the innocuous Exchange Variation of the Ruy Lopez game against Capablanca in the finals of the St. Petersburg tournament in 1914, outmaneuvering the great Cuban, and winning the game. A key moment in the game came at Move 12:

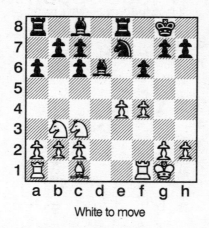

White to move

Instead of completing development and playing for the expected e4-e5 pawn break, Lasker chose to befuddle his opponent by taking over the light squares in the center, even relieving Black of his doubled pawns to do it:

1. f5 b6 2. Bf4 Bb7 3. Bxd6 cxd6 4. Nd4 5. Rad8 Ne6

For the rest of the game the knight remained on e6, until it was time to play the winning combination.

♟ ♞ ♜ ♛

Keep your opponent guessing. Surprises are often hard to deal with.

Principle 117: Don't be intimidated by a high rating or strong reputation.

Ratings and reputations were built yesterday. However strong your opponent may be, she will still have to play well in order to defeat you. That is, if you come to the board with the "show me" attitude. If you are intimidated, you will lose quickly, adding to the reputation of the other guy while showing yourself to be a weakling.

Always force your strong opponent to give you a good, solid lesson in how to play well by playing as well as you can. That way, if you lose, you gained something in compensation. Also, that is the only way you will have a chance to forge another result.

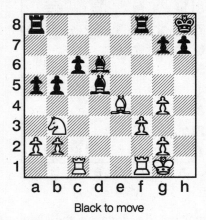

Black to move

This position occurred in a Buffalo simultaneous exhibition given by GM Gata Kamsky. My famous opponent, no doubt distracted by the other games, missed a key tactical element in the position after:

1. ... Bxe4 2. fxe4 Bf4 3. Rc3

This takes the e3-square away from my bishop. But that leaves open:

3. ... Bh2+ 4. Kxh2 Rxf1

Black wins the Exchange (GM Gata Kamsky-Kurzdorfer, simultaneous exhibition, 1991).

♟ ♞ ♜ ♛

Upsets happen in all competitive activities. But you will never pull one off if you come to the board already beaten.

Principle 118: Don't take your opponent too lightly.

This one is the inverse of Principle 117. It is especially relevant when you are the higher ranked or rated player, or you are playing somebody whose play you don't respect. You must always keep in mind that the opponent you don't respect is perfectly capable of finding moves that you must respect.

It is so easy to sit back and relax when you are expected to win. The game will run its course, you figure, and you will win almost without effort. But when you think this way, you're forgetting what made you the favorite in the first place; namely, hard work and concentration before the game and during the game. Each position has to be assessed on its merit, not on the dubious expectation that your opponent is weak so you will see some weak moves. With that attitude, they will come all right—from you!

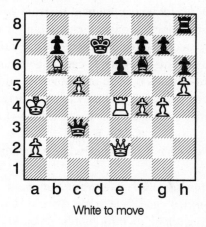

White to move

In a game for first place in a local tournament, the father of one of my students has played at least as well as I have (Kurzdorfer-Frank Grabowski, N. Tonawanda, NY, 1987), despite his ranking four classes below me. The clues are all there. First, he's playing for first place. Second, my king is horribly exposed on a4. Third, the only real threat is for Black's rook to enter the game via the a-file. The play went:

1. Qd1+ Kc8 2. Qe2 Kd7

At this point discretion dictates a repeat of the position with 3. Qd1+ and a sigh of relief that I weathered Frank's break-out tournament. Instead, we get:

3. Qb5+ Ke7

Now there is no longer any way to prevent the Black rook from triumphantly entering play on a8, and Black went on to win.

The only justification for trying to win a drawn position was the relative ranking of the players. The result (Black won) was as predictable as tomorrow's sunrise.

♟ ♞ ♜ ♛

Every dog has his day. Don't ever think you can win without effort.

Principle 119: Don't let your opponent distract you.

Whether it is finger tapping, constant chattering, or contorted facial expressions, many people develop strange behavioral habits during chess games. Many of these behaviors can be quite distracting. But if you learn to ignore all such outside phenomenon, and concentrate on the task at hand, you will never fall prey to such distractions affecting your play. The battle is going on over the board, nowhere else.

♟ ♞ ♜ ♛

Keep focused on what is important when completing any task.

Principle 120: Don't feel sorry for your opponent.

This is a condition that can affect some naive or too nice people. A defeated opponent can look awfully morose. You know how much it hurts to lose, because you have done so enough yourself.

But resist such sympathetic feelings for your opponent, particularly when he or she is a good friend. Put off such feelings until after the game is over. Otherwise, the sympathetic feelings become nothing more than a distraction that prevent you from finishing the game properly. They could well turn the game around, and the sympathy after the game will have to be directed at you.

♟ ♞ ♜ ♛

Learn to discipline your feelings as well as your thoughts during the game.

Chapter 25

Seeing Ahead

Visualizing possible future positions while looking at something else is one of the most important skills to strive for.

Principle 121: Play blindfold chess every chance you get.
Blindfold chess is playing chess without sight of the board or pieces. The reason this is good for you is that it will train you to "see" positions without a physical board and pieces. This is important because during a game you are not allowed to move the pieces around in order to decide what you want to do. Therefore, any planning or calculating you do during a game must be done in your head.

The purpose of playing blindfold chess at first is not to win or even to play particularly well. You simply want to be able to get through a game keeping the constantly changing positions in your head. That's hard enough, and you may need several passes before you get through a complete game. But the effort will pay off in the long run. Though maybe not so well that it will allow such feats as the following:

White to move

This position (Joseph Blackburne-Dr. William, London, 1871) was one of ten games Blackburne played simultaneously without sight of the board. Here is the finish:

1. Bd2 Bh5 2. Bc3 Rg8 3. f6 Bxg6 4. Nxg6+ Kh7 5. f7, Black resigns.

♟ ♞ ♜ ♛

Once you can play without looking, regular play becomes easier.

Principle 122: Attempt to solve any position you come across, anytime, anywhere.

This is a habit principle. If you are really interested in improving your game, you will take every opportunity to do so. That means trying to solve any position you happen to come across. Practice may not lead to perfection, but it will lead to better results.

I found a nice combination in the following position, but didn't realize at the time that I had seen a similar combination in a master game years before. The combination had become part of my knowledge of chess, even if I didn't overtly remember it.

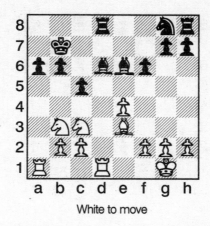

White to move

1. e5 Bc7 2. Rxd8 Bxd8 3. Ne4 Be7 4. Bxc5 Bxb3 5. Bxe7 Bd5 6. Nd6+ Kc6 7. Bf8 and White is winning (Kurzdorfer-Arturo de la Garza, U.S. Class Championship, 1980).

When you are constantly and continually working at something, you are bound to pick up skills you may not even realize you are acquiring.

Principle 123: In figuring out a tactical sequence of moves, choose the candidate moves first. Only then follow them through to their logical outcome, one at a time.

Alexander Kotov gave this advice in *Think Like a Grandmaster*, and it is excellent advice, though very hard to stick with.

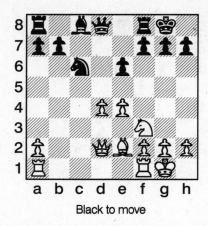

Black to move

Black thinks of breaking up the White center through the move 1. ... e5. Will this work? In order to answer that question, she has to look at A) 13. dxe5 and B) 13. d5.

A) 13. dxe5 Nxe5 14. Qxd8 (not 14. Nxe5? Qxd2) 14. ... Nxf3+ 15. Bxf3 Rxd8, with an even game.

B) 13. d5 Bg4 14. dxc6 Qxd2 15. Nxd2 Bxe2 16. cxb7 Rab8 17. Rfb1 Ba6 ...

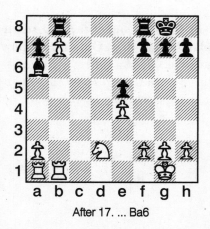

After 17. ... Ba6

and Black recovers her pawn (from the Queen's Gambit Declined, Semi-Tarrasch Variation).

It's another matter altogether how to find all those moves, and how to assess how good they are.

♟ ♞ ♜ ♛

Disciplining your thoughts when following a line of thought is essential if you expect to improve your thinking.

Principle 124: In order to see ahead with any clarity, it is necessary to concentrate on forcing moves (those that change the material or pawn structure of a position).
Captures, checks, pawn promotions, and threats to capture, check, or promote are the forcing moves to concentrate on. Look at the example under Principle 123, and notice how many of the moves were captures or threats to capture. Without this clue, it would be impossible to look ahead even two or three moves.

♟ ♞ ♜ ♛

Help yourself by concentrating on the possibilities that have the most forcing character.

Principle 125: Keep every little detail straight in comparing a position in your head with the one on the board.
This is a big task. You are asked to become Sherlock Holmes, not only seeing what is in front of you, but also noticing every little detail. Then you are asked to notice each little detail throughout every position you look at, even though all those positions are different from what you are looking at. Difficult? Yes, in the extreme. But if chess were easy, would you bother reading a book about it?

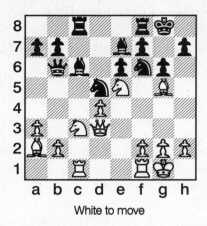

White to move

A grandmaster looked at this position and thought the best play for White is 1. Nxc6 bxc6 2. Bxd5 cxd5 3. Bxf6 Bxf6 4. Nd7, moving a knight that is already gone (from *Thought and Choice in Chess* by Adrianus de Groot). So don't feel bad if you can't see every little detail of every position you look at: Even the best players don't always manage to do it. But do strive for such perfection!

Attention to detail may be more important than any other factor in determining how strong a player you become.

Chapter 26

Courage

"The chess master must have courage, a killer instinct, stamina, and arrogance."

—Larry Evans

"Truth derives its strength not so much from itself as from the brilliant contrast it makes with what is only apparently true."

—Emanuel Lasker

It's not necessarily bad to fear your opponent, his moves, or any of his ideas. But you need to face those fears squarely and not give in to them.

Principle 126: Have the courage of your convictions.

If you believe a sacrifice is correct, you must play it, whether you can calculate it through to its end or not. If you do not, you will be constantly singing the poor song of "If only I had gone ahead with my original idea . . ." Of course, fortune often favors the brave, even the foolishly brave. The following position is a case in point:

White to move

Black has an extra pawn, the bishop pair, and a solid kingside. But there is a chance to break into the Black kingside, and White goes for it, though it means sacrificing a rook.

1. Nf6+ Bxf6 2. Rxf6 gxf6 3. Qxf6 Qa5

Black misses the winning 3. ... Rfe8 4. Bxh7+ Kf8.

4. Re5 Qxe5 5. Qxe5

and White went on to win, though the position is essentially equal (Kurzdorfer-Marshall Dieteman, N. Tonawanda, NY, 1988).

♟ ♞ ♜ ♛

Do what you believe in. The worst that can happen is that you will lose, and you just might win.

Principle 127: Play those positions you know, even if you think your opponent knows more about them.

You're up against a much stronger player, and she is known to be an expert in your favorite defense. Do you switch to another scheme, in the hope of confusing her, or do you stick with your favorite defense?

Think it through. If your opponent is a much stronger player than you are, who do you think will be confused when you play something that you don't know as well? You, of course. Your strong opponent probably knows more about anything you can throw at her. So stick with what you know. In either case, the worst that can happen is that you lose the game. If you played your favorite defense, you could learn something more about it from such an expert. Don't pass up the opportunity for a great lesson in your favorite defense!

Take a free lesson any time you can, and learn from it. This is a great way to improve.

Principle 128: Inferior positions are actually the easiest to play.
The reason is simple. What have you got to lose? The worst that can happen is that you lose the game. If you are already lost, or even just inferior, without many prospects for play, any ideas you get can be tried without too much worry. If it turns out that the idea loses, so what? At least you gave yourself a chance.

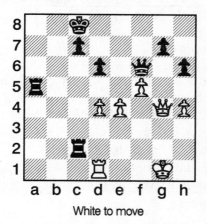

White to move

Down a full rook for nothing, White could have resigned long ago with a clear conscience. Instead, we get:

1. e5 dxe5 2. dxe5 Qxe5

With 2. ... Rxe5 Black slams the door shut and White has nothing left to play for. Of course, Black is still winning after the move played

(2. ... Qxe5), but why give the other guy a chance?

3. f6+ Kb7 4. Qf3+ Rc6

Why walk into a pin voluntarily? The moves 4. ... Ka7 or 4. ... c6 win easily enough.

5. f7

after 5. f7

5. ... Qf5

Black still can win by playing 5. ... Qc5+, but this requires some calculation. Now the game turns completely around.

6. f8=Q Qc2 7. Qb4+ Ka6 8. Qf1+, Black resigns (Kurzdorfer-Ed Schmidt, N. Tonawanda, NY, 1987).

When the pressure is off because you are in deep trouble anyway, you may as well do whatever you like. When there's nothing to lose, imagination flourishes.

Principle 129: Don't offer a draw to a superior player when you are winning, unless a draw secures a big prize.

If the stronger player accepts the draw, you will have lost a big chance to defeat a big gun. These chances don't come up all that often.

Put your ability on the line. If you fail, you will know you at least tried.

Principle 130: Unless you stand to gain big-time, don't offer or accept a draw early in the game or any time there are chances for both sides, regardless of how strong your opponent is or which color you have.

There's more to chess than points or half-points. If these points and your rating are all that matters, your chess life is a poor one indeed. Play the game! That's the reason you're sitting at the board in the first place, isn't it?

♟ ♞ ♜ ♛

If you love being competitive, then compete. Resting on past accomplishments won't ever offer you anything new.

Chapter 27

Opportunity

When opportunity knocks, the good player seizes it.

Principle 131: There are no signposts such as "White to play and win" during a game to alert you.
The only signposts in a chess game are hidden in the position; it is up to you to discover when they are there and what they say. You will not do this unless you are constantly on the alert for the clues—every move of every game. Take the following position, for instance:

Black to move

Black has set up a stone wall defense, which requires moving a lot of pawns. The strength is in Black's control of the light squares in the center, particularly e4. Such games often take on a slow, maneuvering character.

But White has three minor pieces developed to good squares, and his queen is contesting those light squares (if 1. ... Nbd7 2. cxd5 exd5 White wins a pawn with 3. Qxf5). It seems that Black should catch up in development before trying to deploy any more pieces on ideal squares. Therefore, 1. ... Be7 seems to be called for. But the game continued:

1. ... h6 2. Bxf6 Qxf6

Now the label is there, plain for all who understand, that a big lead in development combined with an undefended enemy bishop on a shielded c-file should add up to an excellent game for White. And indeed, he wins a pawn with

3. cxd5

since 3. ... exd5 or 3. ... cxd5 are met with 4. Nxd5 (Kurzdorfer-Wayne Gradl, Buffalo, 1990).

♟ ♞ ♜ ♛

You have to pay attention to every little detail if you want to understand what is really going on.

Principle 132: Be on the alert at all times for opportunities in any game that you play. They come up when least expected.
If this sounds suspiciously similar to the last principle, it is. But you will never answer opportunity's knock if you don't hear it.

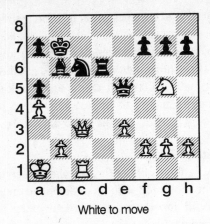

White to move

White has been desperately trying to get something for his piece without too much luck. Black has all his pieces in play and now threatens to trade queens or win another piece. But this is precisely the position where the opportunity lies! Black's last move (... Qe6-e5), which produced those two very potent threats, opened the door for a fantastic combination involving Zwischenzugs, or in-between moves.

1. Nxf7, Black resigns.

All of a sudden it's White who has the threats. Black was counting on 1. Qa3 Rf6 or 1. Qxe5 Nxe5, when f7 is guarded. Or perhaps he thought he could answer the move played (1. Nxf7) with 1. ... Qxc3 2. Rxc3 Rf6, with an easy win. Instead, he noticed that 1. Qxc3 is answered by the Zwischenzug 1. ... Nxd6+ and after 2. Kc7 with another Zwischenzug in 2. ... Nb5+. Therefore, all he has left is 1. ... Qf6 2. Nxd6+ Qxd6 3. Qxg7+ and a lost position (Kurzdorfer-Greg Henry, Bradford, PA, 1990).

♟ ♞ ♜ ♛

Expect opportunities to come up. Look for them, work for them, and whenever they arise, be prepared to take advantage of them.

Principle 133: Strike while the iron is hot.

This is such a well-known saying that it doesn't even appear in quotes. Of course, it is always great advice. As always, the key is in knowing when "the iron is hot." Then knowing when to strike will occur to most competent players.

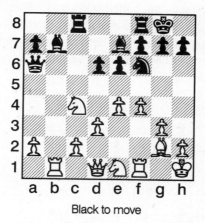

Black to move

White seems to have the better center, but that knight on c4 is a bit precarious, and the knight on e1 is in the way of his rooks. Meanwhile, Black has the bishop pair and some well-placed pieces. But all that won't matter if Black can't find a way to bring his pieces to life and take advantage of White's rather awkward knights.

The opportunity is there. It is not an opportunity for a checkmating attack, to be sure, or even to win material. Black needs to build on what he already has and further disturb White's position. The play goes:

1. ... Bxe4

The support of that c4-knight is knocked out. Black is even willing to part with the bishop pair for the chance to destroy White's pawns, which is just what happens.

2. dxe4 Qxc4 3. Rb7 Rfe8

White's pawns are isolated and exposed. Black went on to win (Bem Tyehimba-Kurzdorfer, Buffalo, 1989).

Pounce when the time is ripe. It is likely that you will not get another chance anytime soon.

Principle 134: Don't get bogged down so much in little details that you miss the bigger picture.

You have to understand the general outline of a game and what plans are possible before you can begin looking for individual moves and calculating variations. Otherwise what are your moves and variations based on? If they are to have any real meaning, they have to be based on the needs of the position.

Black to move

Black was obsessed with a neat little maneuver that had worked in many previous games in similar-seeming positions: Simply get the g8-knight to f7 by playing ... f7-f6 and follow up with ... Ng8-h6-f7.

But the position you see is one in which White has a large lead in development. That means he wants to open the game up. Black simply cannot afford an open game with so many undeveloped pieces. The obvious way to repair Black's problem of retarded development is to get new pieces into the game as fast as possible. The position therefore calls for 1. ... Bg7 or 1. ... Nf6. Instead, we get:

1. ... Nh6

Black was worried about the reply 2. Qd2 if he didn't play this move right away. The battery then stops Black from ever executing his little ... Nh6-f7 maneuver. So the move played (1. ... Nh6) prepares to meet 2. Qd2 with 2. ... Ng4.

But none of this has anything to do with what is actually going on, and White couldn't care less about Black's intricate maneuvers, because he simply opens the game up and wins Black's e-pawn with:

2. dxe5 dxe5 3. Nxe5

Capturing the knight loses to the skewer 3. ... Qxe5 4. Bd4 (Greg Henry-Kurzdorfer, Bradford, PA, 1988).

♟ ♞ ♜ ♛

Don't fail to see the forest for the trees.

Chapter 28

Trust

"Measure the cloth seven times before cutting it once."
—Russian proverb

You have to trust in your own analysis and your own ideas. If you don't, who will? At the same time, be wary of anyone else's analysis. Check it yourself, no matter how esteemed the source.

Principle 135: Trust your intuition—it's usually right.
If you look at a position without doing any intricate analysis, you can usually get a feel for which side has the better chances, or at least where or in which element each side's chances lie. The pieces won't deceive you.

If one side has a bunch of pieces in the center and there are open lines while the other side is cramped, you know enough to start looking for a winning combination. If one side has lots of space and pieces to back it up on the kingside while the other side has a similar advantage on the queenside, you know where each side will likely find play.

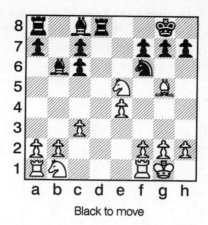

Black to move

White has won a pawn and threatens to win another one on c6. In addition, Black's knight is pinned to his rook, and so is seemingly inactive. But all of this is illusion.

Black can't possibly be worried. It is his move, and he has a lead in development, complete control over the d-file, and a very powerful bishop pair, each of which commands important open diagonals. This is all easy to see after the next few moves.

1. ... Ba6 2. Re1 Nxe4

Black not only doesn't care about the pin, he also scoffs at White's rook on e1, since capturing the knight will get White's king checkmated on the first rank.

3. Bxd8 Bxf2+ 4. Kh1 Bxe1

It is White who has to recover a pawn while still behind in development.

5. Bxc7 Rc8 6. Ba5

Oh, and Black still has those powerful bishops. Black went on to win (Richard Benjamin-Kurzdorfer, Washington, DC, 1990).

♟ ♞ ♜ ♛

You have to trust your intuition. That way, you can learn to correct it whenever it turns out to be wrong.

Principle 136: Check all of your analysis a second time.

It's not practical to check it seven times during a game when the clock is ticking. You'll lose on time before making your winning combination. But do try to recheck your analysis, particularly if it involves material sacrifices. Otherwise some stupid little hallucination or oversight could destroy all your hard work.

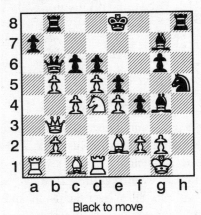

Black to move

White's last move was Nf3xd4. Obviously he wants to answer 1. ... exd4 with 2. Bxg4 and 1. ... Bxe2 with 2. Nxe2. Black calculated three lines:

A) 1. ... exd4 2. Bxg4 Ng3 3. fxg3 d3+, winning.

B) 1. ... Bxe2 2. Nxe2 Ng3 3. Nxg3 fxg3 4. Be3 and White wins.

C) 1. ... Ng3 (forcing White's reply because of the mate threat) 2. fxg3 Bxe2 3. Rd2 exd4 4. Rxe2 d3+, winning.

Of course, line B can be thrown out, and the choice is between lines A and C. Black went with line A because it looked simpler. But a careful check of the variation would reveal the surprise move White found. Line C was forced all the way, even if there were more variations. The game continued:

1. ... exd4 2. Bxg4 Ng3 3. Bh3

blocking the h-file and the mate threats. The game has turned in

White's favor. He went on to win readily (Eric Grabowski-Kurzdorfer, N. Tonawanda, NY, 1987).

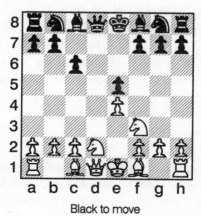

If there's time, always check anything you are planning to do. You could catch a big error before it happens.

Principle 137: Check for yourself any published analysis you are relying on using.

Many tournament players have floundered by relying on the printed word. Chess books are wonderful, and they are filled with more moves, variations, and assessments than anyone can assimilate in one lifetime. But they are written by fallible human authors, and checked by fallible human editors. Mistakes are bound to crop up. So relying on a printed variation to be authoritative without checking it carefully is little different from playing the roulette wheel. The analysis might be right, or it might be refutable.

Black to move

Black can play 1. ... Bc5, which was given in the theory books on this opening some years ago as Black's equalizing move. The books went on to give the reason White can't safely take the e5-pawn: After 2. Nxe5 Bxf2+ 3. Kxf2 Qd4+ 4. Ke1 Qxe5, Black has recovered the pawn and White can no longer castle. But after 5. Nc4,

after 5. Nc4

Black is all of a sudden confronted with an ugly choice: Take the e-pawn and get crushed by 5. ... Qxe4+ 6. Be2 Qxg2 7. Nd6+ Kf8 8. Bf3 Qh3 9. Nf5 (Kurzdorfer-Barry Davis, Buffalo, 1984) or succumb to something like 5. ... Qe6 6. Nd6+ Ke7 7. Nf5+ Kf8 8. Qd8+ Qe8 9. Qxe8+ Kxe8 14. Nd6+, and the fork on f7 and c8 wins material for White.

The book theory overlooked the fact that White's bishop pair, open lines, exposed Black king, and lead in development were more important factors than his having lost the right to castle.

♟ ♞ ♜ ♛

No authority is infallible.

Principle 138: Combinations and complicated tactical play will usually turn out in favor of the side with the sounder position.

This only stands to reason. If your position is sound, any combinations likely to arise will not hurt you. If such a tactical opportunity exists (that will turn the tables in your opponent's favor), then that is a measure of unsoundness in your position.

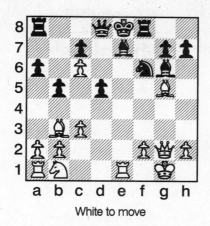

White to move

White is better developed and his long-range pieces control the open board, while Black's king is stuck in the middle and his bishop is pinned. White should therefore look for a combination, since it is likely to turn in his favor.

1. Bxd5 Qd6

Black decided not to call White's bluff. After 1. ... Nxd5 2. Qxd5 Qxd5 3. Rxe7+ Kd8 4. Rd7+ Kc8 5. Rxd5, White gets his queen back along with the extra piece he picked up.

2. Nd2

The same combination is still "on," so White brings more pieces into the game.

2. ... 0-0-0 3. Be6+ Kb8 4. Nb3

White went on to win with his extra pawn and greater control of space (Kurzdorfer-Stanley Elowitch, correspondence game, 1982).

♟ ♞ ♜ ♛

Good things happen to those who follow sound principles.

Chapter 29

Mistakes

"The blunders are all there on the board,
waiting to be made."
—Savielly Tartakower

"In life we are all duffers."
—Emanuel Lasker's *Lasker's Manual of Chess*

"You always learn when people beat you, 'cause you pay
attention and find out why."
—Ray Charles

Nobody plays mistake-free chess for very long—not even the best players. So be prepared to deal with mistakes: Jump on those your opponent makes, keep your own to a minimum, and learn from those you do make.

Principle 139: Don't be afraid of making mistakes. They are inevitable. Rather, get in the habit of learning from them.
This holds true not only after the game is over, but also during play. Usually you will become aware of your mistakes after your opponent has pointed them out by making a strong move. But sometimes you can sense it coming even before that happens. Occasionally, you

won't realize you made a mistake until much later.

In all cases, make your moves boldly. Play as if you know what you are doing, even if you don't. After all, what's the worst that can happen? You make a mistake and lose. So you learn from it and do not make the same mistake ever again.

But if you are afraid to make a mistake, you won't ever take a chance on that combination you think might work, but are afraid of because you can't see everything. That way you will never give yourself a chance to improve, and you will wind up making mistakes anyway!

♟ ♞ ♜ ♛

Trust your ideas and plunge right in. If you are wrong, you will learn from the experience.

Principle 140: Mistakes tend to come in bunches.

This is partly because mistaken moves are bound to come out of mistaken plans and ideas. The mistake may not be apparent right away. This is something to be aware of any time you follow through on your plan.

It is also because we tend to become discouraged after noticing that we made a mistake. Instead of shaking it off, we continue to play out of disgust or despair, and that usually leads to more mistakes.

♟ ♞ ♜ ♛

Be aware of this tendency of mistakes to come in bunches and fight against it.

Principle 141: After you've made a mistake, take some extra time to calm yourself and reassess the position.

This is particularly important in view of Principle 140. By taking extra time to regroup your thoughts, you have a good chance to break the tendency to make multiple mistakes and hold the mistakes to a minimum.

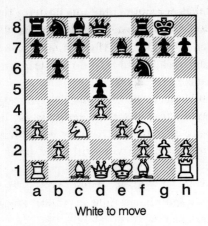

White to move

In the game Kurzdorfer-Cyrus Lakdawala (San Diego match, 1982), play went:

1. Bd3 c5 2. 0-0 Bg4 3. h3 Bh5

I did not like the pin on my f3-knight, and wasn't sure if the discomfort was caused by 1. Bd3 or 2. 0-0, or if I made a mistake at all. But I thought it would be better to immediately break the pin, even if it involved losing a tempo with the bishop.

4. Be2 Nc6 5. g4 Bg6 6. Ne5

It turns out my bishop is actually placed better on e2 than it was on d3. So taking the extra time on the bishop retreat turned out to be very useful.

♟ ♞ ♜ ♛

Taking extra time to rethink your plans after making a mistake is sometimes a game-saving device. In any case, don't just plunge ahead and make more mistakes.

Principle 142: Don't overlook subtle mistakes, such as taking too much or too little time for a move, carelessness in researching your openings or opponent, failing to eat right or get enough sleep, and so on.

Most of the mistakes we notice have to do with the moves of the pieces and the pawns. But of course there's so much more to the game. If you regularly make mistakes on nonchess aspects of your game, well, you know what you have to work on.

♟ ♞ ♜ ♛

We are human beings, with all that entails. We are not robots, or automated calculating computers. Keep your humanness and that of your opponent in mind at all times.

Principle 143: Don't ever expect your opponent to make a mistake.
This is about the worst sin you can commit during a chess game. Your plans and moves must always be made by taking into consideration the best play on your opponent's part. Otherwise how can you expect to win? If you build your plans around poor replies by your opponent, you will only defeat weak players, and then only occasionally.

On the other hand, there is nothing wrong with encouraging your opponent to make a mistake, aiming your play against his best reply, but having a nasty surprise in store in case of a natural mistake.

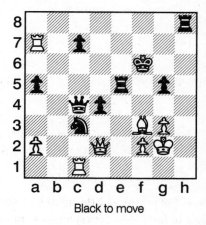

Black to move

Black played the retreat 1. ... Qe6 to double up on the e-file and threaten the check on h3. It doesn't hurt that the natural reply 2. Qxd4 loses immediately to 2. ... Qh3+ 3. Kg1 Ne2+. Other moves, though not losing immediately, still leave White in a difficult position (Greg Henry-Kurzdorfer, Bradford, PA, 1990).

♟ ♞ ♜ ♛

Give your opponent some credit. Even if she happens to be a weak player, her moves could prove to be strong.

Chapter 30

Reaction

How you react to the changing situations during a chess game reveals how good a player you are.

Principle 144: Transition positions (from the opening to the middlegame or directly to the endgame, from the middlegame to the endgame) are the most difficult to handle.

This is because you are not sure which phase you are in during a transition. Be particularly careful about keeping the possible plans in mind, and note the quickly changing peculiarities about such positions. If you need to change plans in a hurry, you must be ready to do so at once.

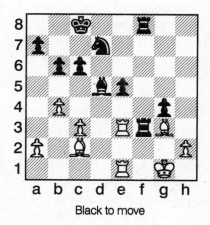

Black to move

Black has been furiously attacking the king, but he is safe now. So the time has come to form a different plan. Black tries for an endgame with an outside passed pawn.

1. ... Rxe3 2. Rxe3 Bxa2 3. Bd1 Be6 4. Bxe5 Nxe5 5. Rxe5 Kd7 6. Kg2 Rf5 7. Rxe6 Kxe6 8. Bxg4

White has got the pawn back and is getting the Exchange back, but:

8. ... a5, White resigns.

There is no way to stop the runaway freight train on the a-file (Ron Burnett-Kurzdorfer, Buffalo, 1995).

♟ ♞ ♜ ♛

Some of the hardest times we go through are when we are between jobs, homes, or mates. Transition times are always difficult.

Principle 145: React to an unexpected, strong move by reassessing the position calmly.

This is how you should react when making mistakes. This is not a coincidence. Anything which is unexpected, whether it is something you or your opponent did, either extra strong or extra weak, needs extra attention. An unexpected strong move from an opponent needs to be looked at very critically, or you could go down in short order.

Look at the figures on pages 96 and 97 in Principle 70 for an example of reacting to a strong move without that extra time and reassessment. Enough said.

♟ ♞ ♜ ♛

Anything unexpected means you didn't take it into account earlier. So you have to take it into account now, or all is lost.

Principle 146: React to any major change in the position by reassessing the position calmly.

A major change, whether expected or not, means new plans are likely going into effect. This usually requires extra time and effort on your part—especially if you expect to take all the details into account and get a plan together that can accommodate everything that is going on.

Look at the figures on pages 128 and 129 in Principle 93 for an example of a major change in position and a subsequent formulating of a new plan.

♟ ♞ ♜ ♛

Any major change demands extra time and reassessment. Never approach these times of change as if nothing has happened or you will not succeed very often.

Principle 147: Know the difference between a strategic position and a tactical position, and react to each accordingly.

The plans need to be very different in each type of position. A wide-open position with active pieces everywhere needs a tactical treatment, while a closed position needs to be milked for whatever positional advantage you can find.

For an example of an open, tactical game with an appropriate plan, see Principle 32 and the figure on page 45. For an example of a closed position with strategic treatment, see Principle 86 and the figure on page 119.

♟ ♞ ♜ ♛

Knowing the type of fight you have before you will help a great deal in conducting the struggle.

Chapter 31

Fighting Spirit

Your capacity for imposing your will on positions may be the most critical skill you can foster.

Principle 148: Nobody ever won a game by resigning.

This one is another very obvious principle. Yet some famous masters have been known to resign in a winning position. Of course, in every case the discouraged loser could not find the winning line, probably because he didn't believe it was there and therefore didn't look for it.

You need look no further than Principle 128 and the figures on pages 169 and 170 to see that continuing to fight in a hopelessly lost position can occasionally pay off. And why not fight on? The worst that can happen is that you will lose, which you will definitely do if you give up.

Where there's life, there's hope. So it is in life, and so it is in chess as well.

Principle 149: The hardest game to win is a won game.

This is a natural corollary to Principle 128, and for the same reason. The defeated opponent is playing with no pressure. She's lost anyway, so what can happen that hasn't already happened? So she fights on with inspiration and imagination. But the player with the winning position knows he has to be precise. One little slip up and he is no longer winning. So the pressure is all on the player on top.

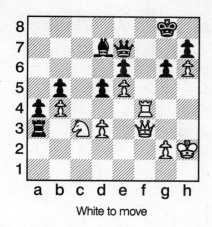

White to move

Although down a pawn, with that passed a-pawn staring him in the face, White has a winning position. He controls the center and has a combination that fatally exposes the Black king. And all the time, that Black rook is powerless to come to the aid of (his) monarch.

1. Nxd5 exd5 2. Qxd5+ Qe6 3. Qc5 Qe8 4. e6 Bxe6 5. Qe5 Qd7

It's time to cash in. White wants to checkmate on g7, and the Black queen is defending. So White should drive the queen off with 6. Rd4 Qe7 7. Rd8+ and the game is his. Except that White thought a direct threat on f8 was the clincher.

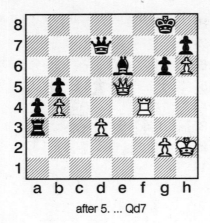

after 5. ... Qd7

6. Qf6 Bf5

That was a move that never occurred to White. The win is gone, and the game is lost, since White gave up a piece to get the winning position in the first place (Kurzdorfer-Mr. McCalmout, Pittsburgh, 1993). Sometimes chess can be so frustrating.

♟ ♞ ♜ ♛

The pressure is on high when you are expected to succeed. This is the hardest road to travel, but also the most rewarding—when you keep the pressure under control.

Principle 150: Physical stamina is sometimes more important in chess than knowledge or analytical ability.

Thinking is not generally thought of as a physical activity, but the brain is certainly physical, and those neurons need to keep firing rather constantly during a long game. So it needs a good, continuous blood supply. Physical fatigue can ruin your game just as sure as poor planning or mistaken calculations.

♟ ♞ ♜ ♛

Make sure you are in good physical shape. Eat properly and exercise. It will enhance everything you do.

Principle 151: **Try to get the most you can from any position, at any time.**

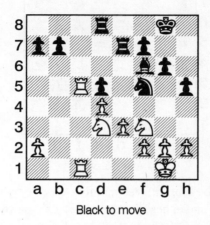

Black to move

White has a central pawn majority and control of the c-file. So how can Black possibly win? By staying alive, defending the threats, and playing to exchange off the rooks, Black will wind up in a superior endgame with an outside pawn majority. This is easier said than done, and it has to be carried out one move at a time.

1. ... Kf8 2. Nf4 Red7 3. g3 Ng7 4. Rb5 Ne6 5. Nd3 b6 6. Rb2 Rc7 7. Rxc7 Nxc7 8. Rc2 Ne6 9. a4 Be7 10. Kg2 f6 11. Rc6 Kf7 12. Nh4 Rd6 13. Nb4

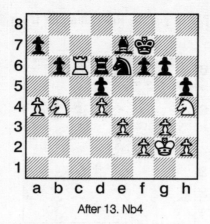

After 13. Nb4

Black has to be careful. Trading rooks on c6 now will run into 13. ... Rxc6 14. Nxc6 and either Black's a-pawn or g-pawn will fall.

13. ... Rd7 14. Nd3 Rc7 15. Rxc7 Nxc7

Black has finally carried out the plan and now has the better game (Mike Aaron-Kurzdorfer, Buffalo, 1984). Of course, the play wasn't forced, and White perhaps could have made more of the c-file, not allowing the rook exchanges.

♟ ♞ ♜ ♛

Success is never guaranteed. But always striving for success greatly increases your chances.

Principle 152: Don't give up the game until there's nothing left to play for.

How many times have you had a completely winning position, lost interest in the game (since the position would obviously win itself), and gone on to lose as a result? How many times has your opponent fallen for the same insidious temptation?

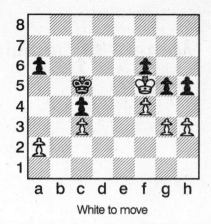

White to move

In this position, the simplest way to win is to exchange pawns on g5 and then dine on the g- and h-pawns. But White, who had been trading down to this winning endgame for some time, simply took a free pawn with 1. Kxf6, expecting his opponent to resign. Instead, after 1. ... h4!, it was White who had to resign, since Black will get a new queen in all variations, while the White pawns will not make it to the eighth rank (Kurzdorfer-Neil Goldberg, Buffalo, 1983).

When success is near, there is a natural tendency to relax. After all, we have paid our dues; all our hard work is about to be rewarded.

This is a very dangerous time. We so easily forget what got us this far. The hard work, preparation, and concentration that went into our near success must continue to the end if we are to experience complete success. This is no time to get lazy! The old farm saying "don't count your chickens before they are hatched" came from a potential chess champion.

"It ain't over 'til it's over."

—Baseball legend Yogi Berra

Chapter 32

The Moment of Decision

"Thou shalt not shilly-shally!"
—Aron Nimzovich

The moment when you must make a decision arrives whether you want to recognize it or not. It's probably best to recognize it.

Principle 153: Make your decision, then live or die with it.
Don't torture yourself with a lot of "coulda, woulda, shouldas." There is plenty of time for recrimination after the game is over. During play, you must live with whatever decisions you have already made. Otherwise your mind will not be on the task at hand.

In some situations you can move a piece to where it used to be, but most of the time to do so simply loses time. Unless this is the only way to avoid further deterioration of your position, it's best to plunge ahead with your plan.

A great example of this principle is illustrated here.

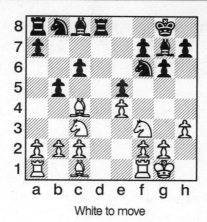

White to move

White has committed his light-square bishop to the a2-g8 diagonal, so backing up with 1. Bd3, in order to save the e-pawn after 1. ... b4 2. Ne2 doesn't make a lot of sense.

White must follow through with aggressive moves. The play thus included a piece sacrifice, aimed at exposing the Black king.

1. Bb3 b4 2. Nxe5 bxc3

Black could also back out with 2. ... Be6 3. Bxe6 fxe6 4. Ne2 Nxe4 5. Nd3, but he has also committed himself—to winning a piece.

3. Nxf7 Rf8 4. Nd6+ Kh8 5. bxc3

♟ ♞ ♜ ♛

White has three pawns for the piece and has a powerful, passed e-pawn. This is certainly at least sufficient compensation for the piece (Kurzdorfer-Milo Friedenburg, Los Angeles, 1980).

♟ ♞ ♜ ♛

Analyze the consequences of taking alternate paths before making any decision.

Principle 154: When you see a good move, wait. Don't play it. Look for a better move.

This principle applies as long as there is no shortage of time. When the clock is ticking, however, and you are running low on time, forget about this principle. Finding a better move after you have run out of time will never do you any good.

When there is plenty of time, however, why not give it some extra thought when the move you are about to make looks very good. You might have a forced win.

A great example is shown in the figure on page 175 from Principle 133. Black had good enough moves in 1. ... d5 or 1. ... Rfd8 available. But these don't punish White for placing his knight so awkwardly on c4. The good-enough moves aren't attempts to win the game, and that's what chess is all about.

♟ ♞ ♜ ♛

Don't rush forward with a move that's good enough unless you have to. It's usually better to take time to think your plans through. That way, you can get the maximum out of your position.

Principle 155: Spend some extra time on an important decision, when the result of the game is on the line. There's no sense rushing now.

If the previous principles haven't brought this truth home already, here it is now. To play quickly when the game is on the line is the height of folly. How can you be sure you are playing the best move, or finding the best plan, or digging out the best combination if you just reach out and play the first move you see?

A great example of this principle in action is the thinking behind the plan shown in Principle 93 and illustrated by the figures on pages 128 and 129. This planning did not appear out of thin air. It was based on the pieces and pawns as they appeared in the position, and took into account many possibilities. This is not something you want to come up with in a few seconds.

♟ ♞ ♜ ♛

Take your time to think it through, and you will have a high degree of success.

Chapter 33

Using Time

The time you have to think about your moves is usually very limited. Learn to use this time wisely.

Principle 156: **Stay out of time-pressure situations unless they are your bread and butter.**

This is becoming harder and harder to do in tournament games these days. Time limits are becoming shorter for various reasons. Players want to get the maximum amount of games played in the minimum amount of time, and promoters are trying to involve spectators through television or the Internet.

Nevertheless, you can do your best to stay out of time-pressure situations by allocating an average amount of time per move. If the time limit is an hour per game per player, you are not doing yourself any favors by taking thirty minutes to make one move, unless it has a chance to win the game for you. The average time per move should be something like one minute.

If the time limit is half an hour per player per game, a ten-minute think is likely to come back to haunt you at the end of the game. Your average think should be something like thirty seconds.

Use your time wisely. You should never forget Principles 154 and 155, even in a fast time-limit game. Just remember to use a relatively larger slice of time in the critical situations and in searching for a win when you suspect one to be there.

Using time wisely is not commonplace. Make it a habit, and your success rate will go up.

Principle 157: Take more time on transition positions and decisive moments.
Once again, this principle applies even to fast time-limit games. The key is in understanding that the phrase "more time" is short for "more time in relation to your other moves." This extra time is relative to the average time you spend on most moves.

The reason we single out transition positions and decisive moments is simply that how you handle these positions will greatly affect your success rate. These positions are more complex than normal, and in general "separate the men from the boys."

If this isn't clear to you, you may need to refer to Principles 102, 144, and 155.

♟ ♞ ♜ ♛

Taking extra time to think when your future is on the line makes a lot of sense. Give the most important decisions their due.

Principle 158: Don't go into a long think over routine moves.
This is directly related to spending more time on transition positions and decisive moments. That extra time won't be available if you think deeply about routine positions. Therefore, use openings you know, and study basic strategies, endgames, and combinations.

Many positions will offer nothing much in the way of combinations or plan formulation. These are positions that have to be played quickly—making routine developing moves aimed at improving your position or routine preventive moves to stop your opponent from opening up the position to your detriment.

The key is, of course, recognizing that nothing special is hidden in these routine positions. This relates intimately to the next principle.

♟ ♞ ♜ ♛

Spend as little time as possible on routine tasks so that you can

take all the extra time you need when the going gets rough or the time
has come for a big decision to be made.

Principle 159: **Rely heavily on intuition rather than calculation
in rapid games.**
Obviously, the reason for this is that if you take the necessary time to
think through your combinations—calculating all the moves and comparing all the resulting positions—you will run out of time before you
ever play your winning move.

Nevertheless, intuition is also important in slow games, in that it
gives you a good idea of which moves to investigate first and which
plans are more likely to work. This principle relates to Principle 135
(trust your intuition). Intuition is the feeling you have about a position,
and it is built over a lifetime of playing chess, playing over the games
of the masters, and attempting to solve any chess position you come
across. If you are just starting out or have not been involved in the
game for very long, your intuition will not be as well developed as
that of the more experienced player, but that is only a temporary state.
So develop your intuition and it will get more reliable as time goes by.

♟ ♞ ♜ ♛

Whenever you must make a quick decision, or whenever you
want to begin the process of making a well-thought-out decision, your
intuition will play a key role. Let it.

Principle 160: **When your opponent is under time pressure, do
not rush your moves to minimize the time she has to think during
your thinking time.**
There is a most curious phenomenon that anybody who has played
chess at various time controls can attest to. Some players simply
cannot budget their time very well, or actually prefer to put themselves in the position of having to make many decisions very quickly.

A time control of two and a half hours for the first forty moves
(for each player), followed by another hour for the next twenty moves,

and yet another for the next twenty moves should be sufficient time for anyone to figure out almost any position. The game can take up to five hours for the first forty moves (2½ hours plus 2½ hours) and can drag on into the night (an extra two hours for the next twenty moves, another two hours for the next twenty moves, etc.), with the possibility of taking a dozen hours or more if the game lasts very long. There are reasons why such time controls are no longer in vogue.

Nevertheless, there were always players who got into severe time-pressure, needing to make twenty moves or more in the last minute to reach Move 40. This is a clear case of failure to budget time well, and many players suffer from it.

So what happens when your opponent is one of these time-pressure addicts? The best advice is to ignore the time pressure, hard as that may be to do. Such players are used to time pressure, and can handle themselves very well, coming up with good plans and good moves in seconds. So if you decide to play their game, blitzing out your moves in the vain hope of making the opponent run out of time, you are merely putting yourself in the same stressful situation your opponent is in.

It is much better to take the time you have saved for your own thinking to think about the situation on the board in a detached way, taking into account only the position and the possible combinations. In other words, continue to play normally. You might think that this is giving your stressed-out opponent valuable extra think time, but actually what you are doing is giving this time to yourself. Your opponent must instantly switch gears as soon as you make your move, which will be when you decide to make it.

In essence, you are actually adding to your opponent's troubles by taking your time, while blitzing moves with her plays right into her hands.

♟ ♞ ♜ ♛

When your resources are greater than those of your opponent, it is foolish to throw them away. Choose to play at your own pace when you can, and force your opponent to play your game.

Chapter 34

Thinking

Whether analytical, logical, or haphazard, your thoughts during a game have a lot to do with how strong a player you are.

Principle 161: Keep your mind on the game.
During a game, do you think thoughts such as "it's awful noisy in here"; "this guy I'm playing is a slob"; "there is a nice combination on the next table; let's see if it will work"; or "my opponent is rated low, so I will have no trouble winning"?

Anything that does not pertain to the position in front of you is extraneous thought; eliminate it. You are trying, presumably, to get the most out of the position you have, and you will not do that by wasting valuable thinking time on frivolous or distracting thoughts.

If disciplining your thinking is too hard and just no fun, then realize that you simply will not be as strong a player as you could be. If your opponent puts everything she has into the game and you do not, then don't be shocked when she defeats you.

Disciplining your thinking is probably the most valuable skill you can cultivate. If you are serious about becoming a strong player, this is something you cannot afford to neglect.

Keeping your mind on the task at hand will bring wonderful rewards in the long run. Come to think of it, it will probably bring rewards in the short run as well.

Principle 162: Focus your chess thinking.

It may be well and good to recommend keeping your mind on the game (Principle 161), but just how can you do that? By finding a focus point and sticking with it.

Your focus will change from game to game and from position to position. It may even change from opponent to opponent. You will have to learn what to focus on during any specific situation by using your intuition (Principles 135 and 159) and trial and error.

The focus point could be the opponent's king, or it could be the center, or an isolated d-pawn. It could be a bad bishop, an out-of-play piece, or your opponent's sudden, possibly unsound, combination. Whatever it is, keep on it, and try to understand what is going on in the game and the position at hand. Do this throughout any game, any time, and your thinking during a game, and quite possibly away from the game, will improve.

♟ ♞ ♜ ♛

By keeping a focus point in mind, otherwise difficult tasks become more possible. An entire project may become more comprehensible, or a plan realizable. Keep a focus point in everything you do.

Principle 163: Compare your position with similar positions you remember.

This is a technique which you will get better at with practice. Comparing positions will not only give you focus points to begin with, but they will also train your memory, and build up a store of familiar positions.

Comparing positions you have before you with positions from your memory is a bit different from the usual technique of comparing the resultant position at the end of a series of moves with other resultant positions at the end of other series of moves. Comparing an actual position with your memory of similar positions is useful because it can improve your understanding of chess. The more positions you understand, the better player you will be.

For example, once you understand the figures on page 21 (Principle 15) and page 110 (Principle 79), you shouldn't have much trouble finding the combination in the figure on page 58 (Principle 41). Exposing the king by way of removing key defenders is an idea that will crop up constantly whenever you or your opponent are involved in a king hunt.

It should be obvious that such ideas are common among strong players. The more of them you understand, the better player you will be.

♟ ♞ ♜ ♛

By comparing the new and unusual with the old and well known, patterns begin to emerge. Pay attention to them, and cultivate more and more of these patterns. That way your knowledge base grows, and you become better equipped.

Principle 164: Think along strategic lines when it is your opponent's turn and along tactical lines when it is your turn.

This principle is a specific way to implement Principles 161 and 162. It also is not and should not be a hard and fast rule, like many of the others. After all, if your opponent plays very fast, you won't get to do much in the way of planning or strategic thinking in a game if you follow this principle too closely. Rather, it is a guide to breaking up your thinking during a game into patterns.

By thinking of specific moves and series of moves when it is your turn to move, you focus on the task at hand, which is to find the best move in the given position.

By thinking of strategic ideas when it is your opponent's turn to move, you make sure your thoughts don't fall off when it is not your turn to move. Getting lazy and not thinking at such times will do nothing more than decrease your chances to pick it up again once it is your move.

Dividing up the thought processes like this is simply a convenient way to keep your brain on all cylinders throughout the game without burning out on straight calculation.

Get into the habit of dividing your thoughts into the specific and the general. Know the difference between the two, and keep them separate. But, don't neglect either one.

Principle 165: Use the question and answer format.
When trying to determine the best move to make during a game, it is often useful to have a dialogue with yourself. For example, take the following position.

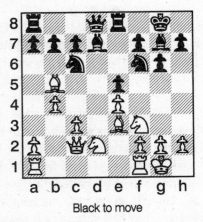

Black to move

Let's say you are playing the Black pieces in this game. The first things you notice are that both sides have a solid center pawn, both sides are safely castled, and both sides are completely developed. Well, White has connected his rooks with his last move (1. Qd1-c2), so that Black is still half a move shy, just like at the beginning of the game.

So you can start asking yourself the following questions:

1. Is there anything else about this position that I should notice?

Answer: White has that pawn on b4, which gives him more space on the queenside and somewhat weakens his pawn structure. Perhaps that information is something you can use.

2. Are all the pieces defended?

Answer: All Black's pieces are defended. But two White pieces—

the b5-bishop and the queen—are not defended. White could have completed his development last move with 1. Qe2 or 1. Qa4. This bit of information can also be significant.

3. Are either of the undefended White pieces vulnerable?

Answer: The bishop on b5 is on the same diagonal with the Black bishop on d7. There is a Black knight in the way.

4. Is there any way we can make use of White's potential weaknesses—that pawn stuck on b4, the undefended, vulnerable b5-bishop—by making a forcing, threatening move?

Answer: Black could play 1. ... Nd4 or 1. ... Nxb4. Both moves attempt to take advantage of the undefended White pieces using a double attack.

So Black begins analyzing variations beginning with those two moves. Since the second move wins a pawn while the first move does not, he chose the second move, and went on to win the game (David Hart-Kurzdorfer, correspondence game, 1981).

Notice that rather normal moves such as 1. ... Qe7 or 1. ... a6 never even came up. When there's a problem with either side, try to find out what it is and how it might be exploited.

♟ ♞ ♜ ♛

Questions and answers can help uncover the truth in any position, provided relevant questions are asked and honest answers are sought.

Chapter 35

Concentration

*"It is not enough just to be a good player;
one must also play well."*

—Siegbert Tarrasch,
after a poor showing in a
Leipzig tournament of 1888

Some players are easily distracted. Others don't seem to notice what goes on around them. Why is that? Basically, some players have better concentration than others do. Be one of the latter.

Principle 166: If you aren't concentrating because of some distraction, perhaps the fault lies with your powers of concentration rather than in the distraction.
Chess is played in noisy, smoky bars and quiet hotel halls where a loud band is booked in the next room. Clubs and informal contests feature kibitzers, while formal tournaments and matches can have potentially noisy audiences. How is a player supposed to concentrate? By practicing to concentrate in adverse conditions, of course.

One time I played a strong German master in a local San Diego club tournament. He was much stronger than I was and, not surprisingly, had a much better position in the late middle game. But the club building was situated in a park and it was a nice, sunny day. An accordion player decided that this was a great time to serenade everyone within earshot. His performance was loud, obnoxious, and bad. But I was used to playing under all sorts of noisy conditions, and the background "music" didn't affect my concentration a bit.

My esteemed opponent felt differently. The awful sounds wafting in were too much. They broke his concentration, and his game began showing signs of wear. He eventually left the door open for counterplay that secured a draw for me.

♟ ♞ ♜ ♛

Distractions abound. Instead of being disturbed by them, isn't it better to concentrate in spite of them?

Principle 167: Find a way to proof yourself against distractions.

I learned this principle from dog training, of all things.

When you want to teach your dog a trick, first you show him what to do, then praise him and give him treats for doing it right. But then you also correct him when he does it wrong.

However if you want the dog to really know the trick, you proof her against distractions. This means you throw a toy out in the path of a dog that is supposed to come straight to you, or you introduce unfamiliar people, dogs, or cats into the sessions. If she can perform well under those conditions, she really knows the trick.

Former World Champion Mikhail Botvinnik had some trouble with cigarette smoke during play, so he went to the extreme measure of training with heavy smokers so he could get used to playing under such conditions.

Perhaps it is not necessary to go to such extremes, but playing under adverse conditions will tend to proof you against getting distracted by anything not directly relating to the game and position at hand. So do it regularly, and learn to concentrate regardless of the distractions.

♟ ♞ ♜ ♛

Practice under worse conditions than you expect, and your ability to concentrate should improve.

Principle 168: Disciplining your thinking will go a long way toward improving your concentration.

This principle links Principles 161 and 162 with Principles 166 and 167. Disciplined thinking leads directly to better concentration.

This is perhaps one of the proofs you can put your concentration to. Try thinking in a methodical way under all sorts of adverse conditions. Play blindfold chess at a party or in a bar. If you can get through a game played with the distractions you will have under such conditions, your concentration must be in pretty good shape.

By concentrating on the method of thinking, on the discipline of the thought process, you will automatically shut out all sorts of distractions. After all, how can you go through a number of move series, compare them, and come to a conclusion while paying attention to small talk or music? Something will have to give; just make sure it isn't your thought process or concentration.

♟ ♞ ♜ ♛

Methodical thinking and good concentration are complementary. Focusing on either one will help the other.

Principle 169: Don't pay any attention to psychological aspects during a game.

Unlike poker, where body language, facial expression, and other outward signs can give away your hand, chess is a game in which the only thing that matters is the position at hand. Thus it is a waste of time and, worse, it may adversely affect your concentration, to pay too much attention to any psychological by-play going on during a game.

It's okay to play to an opponent's known weakness. For instance, one player may be uncomfortable with a wide-open position in which she is forced to attack. So give her such a position. Or play to exchange queens against someone who thinks endgames are boring. But do not spend time reading your opponent's feelings during a game; they will not help you in coming up with a good plan or the best move, and they may mislead you into something that has nothing to do with the position at hand.

In chess, the position is there for all to see. The difference between strong and weak players is in their ability to read what is there in front of both.

♟ ♞ ♜ ♛

Keep your mind on the task at hand. Concentrate on that, and your chances for success will increase.

Play the board, not the player. The best way to psych out an opponent is to always play the strongest moves.

Chapter 36

Patience

All strong players possess this virtue in abundance, at least during a closely contested game. Therefore, it's probably a good idea for you to cultivate this virtue as well.

Principle 170: Sit on your hands.
This admonition is a very practical bit of advice, aimed at those who reach out to play the first move that pops to mind. Most young and beginning players are prone to this habit, and it is a horrible one.

Always remember the standard rule for chess is touch-move. Touch a piece and you must move it. Let it go and your move is completed. There is no take-back in chess, despite that feature in so many chess-playing computers.

It makes no sense to snatch at a piece and quickly move it, only to discover too late that you are making a horrible mistake. It's so much better to think before you move. If you need to literally sit on your hands in order to achieve this good habit, then by all means do so. Some of us only need to figuratively sit on our hands, but one way or another, we should all make sure to think first, and only move after we're sure we have it right.

Think it through first, then take action. Look before you leap. Whoever heard of doing it successfully the other way around?

Principle 171: Be particularly patient with your pawns.

Pawns are peculiar in that they cannot move backward or sideways. Therefore you can never take back a pawn push, no matter how minor a mistake it may have been. The squares the pawn used to protect before it moved will never again be protected by that pawn for the rest of the game.

Therefore any decision to move a pawn is a potentially important one. Thus being patient when contemplating such moves makes a lot of sense.

If it seems that you remember another principle that is similar to this one (Principle 110: When in doubt, do anything but push a pawn), it's only because you are paying good attention to these principles. Consider very carefully whenever thinking of moving a pawn. The move may be very good, but it will always have that "Crossing the Rubicon" flavor.

♟ ♞ ♜ ♛

Be patient with any potentially important decision you may have to make. This doesn't mean don't do anything aggressive or anything that could potentially backfire on you. Rather, it means consider carefully whenever you believe an aggressive action could have unintended consequences down the line. Just make sure you know the potential weaknesses as well as the potential benefits to anything you do.

Principle 172: Be patient while waiting for your opponent to move.

This one catches chess players every day. It is particularly bad in slow time-limit games.

When players think about a move for a long time, many opponents tend to get impatient. But this is the worst possible reaction they can have. Anyone who is thinking for a long time is up to something. Either she is searching for a combination that she hopes will get her out of her difficulties, or she is searching for a good plan, or calculating a possible winning combination. Whatever the outcome of this long think, you can be sure your opponent is attempting to understand the position on a deeper level than you understand it. So, do you get impatient and wish she'd move already, or do you concentrate on the position and look for any hidden resources?

It's a pretty good idea to search just as long and as hard as your opponent if you expect, or hope, to wind up with a win. Therefore, work just as hard as your opponent does on her long think. Who knows, maybe you will discover more than she does. You certainly will not out-think her if you wait impatiently for her to move!

♟ ♞ ♜ ♛

Successful people know how to fill up downtime. They don't waste it. Get into the habit of thinking even when the pressure is not on, and you will be more successful.

Principle 174: Be patient in your calculation.

Don't jump at the first good-looking move. Make sure it checks out, and make sure you look at other likely moves as well. This is the only way to have a chance at coming up with the best move. Calculation is hard work. Keeping the various series of moves, along with the resulting positions in mind, to be called up at will for comparison, takes energy and concentration This is not the time to get lazy and impatient! Stay with it all the way through.

This is a principle to keep in mind not only during the game, but also in any training or analysis sessions. Patience is a learned art, and it's a really good idea to acquire the habit. Calculate patiently any time you calculate, and you will form this habit.

♟ ♞ ♜ ♛

Any long and difficult endeavor requires patience for those who wish to be successful. Calculating possible futures based on reliable data certainly has the potential to be long and difficult. So be patient! Don't expect it all to become clear in a minute.

Principle 175: Be patient in reacting to times of crisis during your games.

This is when the outcome of the game gets decided. The moment of decision (see Chapter 32) is often a time of crisis—when all your hard work comes to fruition or to ruin. There are also times when it looks like everything is going down the drain (Principles 128 and 148). This is not the time to carelessly plunge ahead with something that springs to mind, and maybe might work.

Whenever the game is on the line, for whatever reason, it's probably a very good idea to be aware that this is the case. Once you have identified that a crisis is in full bloom, take extra time and care to make sure you get everything you can from the position. This is probably just the time that a good supply of patience will pay the most dividends.

♟ ♞ ♜ ♛

Successfully managing a crisis situation demands the possession of plenty of patience. With copious supplies of this virtue, your success rate will be marvelous.

Chapter 37

Luck

"There are two classes of men; those who are content to yield to circumstance, and play whist; those who aim to control circumstances, and who play chess."

—Mortimer Collins

If you think luck doesn't play a part in chess, you probably haven't played a whole lot. People who don't know chess usually have the impression that it is entirely a game of skill. This is true up to a point.

While the kind of luck present in gambling games is absent in chess (everybody gets the same amount and array of pieces and pawns; the position is completely visible to all parties at all times), that doesn't mean that luck does not play a part. It is in fact present in many small forms that are not immediately apparent to the inexperienced player.

Principle 176: There are all kinds of situations where luck plays a part in chess.

In a five-round tournament, some players wind up with White in three games, while others get White in only two games. Since it is a small advantage to have the White pieces, this gives the player with more Whites a larger-than-usual advantage. Likewise, if you play White against your most formidable opponents and wind up with Black against the weaker opposition, you are luckier than an opponent who winds up with Black against the strong players and White against the novices.

Color allocation, like most forms of luck in chess, evens out in the long run, but can run for you or against you in the short run.

You may also be lucky if your opponent, who has completely outplayed you, stumbles and blunders away the game just before you were about to resign. This would seem to have very little to do with your skill in playing the game. Of course, the opposite scenario, in which you blunder away a win after completely outplaying your opponent, cannot be put down to bad luck. It is, after all, your responsibility to keep playing well until the game is over.

Other forms of luck in chess have to do with continually coming up against particularly difficult opponents in games that will make or break the tournament for you, or getting into positions that your opponent knows particularly well. You could also count playing moves or positions the book says are winning for you only to find your opponent was aware of a refutation to the book analysis. But that can be attributed less to luck than to your failure to critically analyze the position or move.

These forms of good and bad luck are part of the game, and are taken into account by the discerning player. Although they all tend, like color allocation, to even out in the long run, they can be very annoying or gratifying in the short run. Just keep in mind that luck in chess is present, though mostly as a minor component.

♟ ♞ ♜ ♛

Mortimer Collins notwithstanding, there is a certain amount of luck even in the most skill-oriented activities. We cannot always control the circumstances, no matter how hard we try. I will add that there are two classes of people; those who accept this and those who don't.

Principle 177: Fortune favors the brave.

This well-known platitude is particularly true in chess, where aggression and forthright attacks so often throw the opponent into disarray. At least one reason why this is so is that defending is such a distasteful activity for most players. There are not many good defenders below the master level, and even at that level and above, the courageous attacker often has an advantage over the defender.

This principle helps to explain some of the good luck players have in turning poor or losing positions into winning combinations. It isn't all luck: there is a direct relationship between how aggressively you play when you are losing and your success rate from such situations. The figures on pages 169, 174, and 197 are prime examples of an aggressive player turning a lost position into a win by throwing caution to the winds.

♟ ♞ ♜ ♛

Boldly step forward and perform, regardless of circumstance and criticism. The key is to go boldly, whether or not anyone has done it before. (Sorry, Admiral Kirk.)

Principle 178: The good player makes her own luck.

This is the natural corollary to Principle 177. Since there is luck in chess, the good player recognizes the fact and works to maximize her own good luck, while at the same time attempting to maximize her opponent's bad luck.

Part of this is playing aggressively, part of it is attitude, and part of it is fighting to get the most out of each and every position, regardless of who stands better or who is supposedly the better player. But mostly, it's attitude.

The lucky player is one who makes the most of her opportunities. That means the better you play, the luckier you will be. Good players don't rely on mistakes from their opponents. Rather, they give their opponents chances to go wrong, and are prepared to take advantage of any mistake in their opponent's play, any time, and under any circumstances.

♟ ♞ ♜ ♛

Good things happen to those who follow the way. That's what Tao is all about.

Chapter 38

Practice

*"I was wrong in supposing that I could bottle
up my chess and put it in a glass case."*
—Adolf Anderssen, after his defeat by Paul Morphy in 1858

You will learn to make good decisions by making many decisions. When they turn out badly, you will take note of that and not repeat the same mistakes. When they turn out well, you will take note of that and keep making similar decisions.

Principle 179: Practice makes perfect.
This is the mantra of musicians. It should also be the mantra of anybody who wants to do anything well. Although perfection is rarely attainable, it is something we strive for, in an effort to be as good as possible. But of course this practice has to be based on sound principles.

Playing a lot of chess will not help you at all if you keep making the same mistakes over and over again. Practice only becomes worthwhile when it is accompanied by a critical analysis of each and every performance.

So in order to improve through practice, what is needed is a lot of chess games played against various opponents in different types of positions. That's step one. Step two is to examine every move of every game critically. This step is vital to any hoped-for improvement. Without it, your play is not practice. It is just repetition. There is a huge difference.

Step two is the important part. Critically examining your decisions is what allows you to improve. But of course you cannot do that if you do not make those decisions in the first place. Thus you must play in order to have positions that you have played to critically analyze. This is what practice is all about. Playing and critically examining your play.

♟ ♞ ♜ ♛

Performing is necessary in order to attain proficiency at performance. But critically examining your performance is also necessary if you expect to gain anything from the experience. The package is what gives you the chance to strive for perfection.

Principle 180: Play an opening first, then look up what theory there is on it.

Many players approach this principle the other way around. They study the openings first to discover how they should be played, and then incorporate the opening into their practice.

The trouble with this approach is that you will learn to play many moves by rote, without really understanding what you are doing. There's nothing wrong with memorization per se, but memorizing series of moves without thoroughly understanding them is folly. It is so easy to play the same moves in the same order as the remembered series even if your opponent strays a little. But a different move order from the opponent can change the entire complexion of the game, and what was winning in one position may as easily now lose.

But playing an opening from a fresh perspective, which you necessarily do if you don't know it very well, forces you to think about your moves and come up with good reasons for playing them in the order you choose. Your moves and/or your move order may not be the best available, but at least they will be well thought out. Later, when studying what the masters have done in similar positions, you will discover not only how good your moves were, but also which moves are considered best and, more importantly, why they are considered best.

Learn from trial and error as well as from the advice of the masters (whether from books, other media, or in person). That way you will learn how to think as well as what thoughts are considered appropriate and why they are considered appropriate.

Principle 181: There is nothing that will teach you more than a good drubbing by a strong player.

If you like to win, you can do one of two things. Play weak opponents you know you can defeat, or play strong players in order to learn how to play better from your defeats. The first may be more gratifying to your ego in the short run, but the second will give you much more in the long run.

If you are serious about improving your game, then you will learn more from your defeats than from most of your victories. One reason for this phenomenon is that you can discover what strong players do to win. (You put up the stiffest possible resistance and still lost. Study the game and you will discover what defeated you. Next time, try that strategy yourself.) Another reason is that losing hurts. It doesn't make you feel good or smart. So you will work harder to make sure you do not lose next time. The end result is that you will eventually play up to the level of your opponent.

With that understanding in mind, does it make any sense to continually play those who have nothing to offer you but weak resistance every time you attack?

♟ ♞ ♜ ♛

In any competition, go after the stiffest opposition any time you want to improve. That way, not only will you improve, but when you do win, it will really be meaningful, and show a certain level of expertise.

Principle 182: Always play at your best.

This principle almost goes without saying, except that there are times when we are tempted to play weakly in order to allow our young or inexperienced opponent to have a chance. This is a temptation it is well to resist.

First, playing weakly in such a situation is patronizing. Second, it gives your young or inexperienced opponent a false sense of his ability. Third, any future encounter won legitimately by your opponent becomes devalued. Just like you want to know all your victories are earned, so do your opponents.

In a situation in which there is little point of playing because you are obviously too strong, it's much better to play at your best, but under a handicap. Anything will do, depending on what is appropriate. Take less time on your clock, play blindfolded, or do it the old-fashioned way—take off a pawn, a knight, a rook, or your queen. These old-fashioned odds games had a real purpose, and can still be meaningful in the right situation.

In order to understand this principle better, just think of the opposite situation—in which your opponent is obviously too strong for you to have a chance in a level game. What would you rather have her do? Lose to you by playing weak moves? Or play her hardest? If she doesn't play at her hardest, why bother playing? Just play someone weaker.

♟ ♞ ♜ ♛

Don't play a competitive game unless you are going to play it competitively. There is never a legitimate purpose for playing weak moves on purpose in order to lose.

Principle 183: Practice playing endings if you want to master the intricacies of opening and middlegame positions.

Endgames contain the foundations of good chess play, and are studied the least by most players.

Endgames contain the foundations of good play because they incorporate the simplest positions. How can you truly understand a complicated opening or middlegame position until you understand each endgame it could transpose into? If you don't know how bishops fare against knights in the simplest bishop-and-pawn versus knight-and-pawn endgame, how can you possibly understand a middlegame position featuring bishops, knights, rooks, and queens on each side?

Look at Principle 89 and the figure on page 122 again. This idea of the crippled pawn majority versus a healthy pawn majority comes up in endgames from time to time, and is a big reason for at least one opening variation: The Ruy Lopez Exchange Variation (1. e4 e5 2. Nf3 Nc6 3. Bb5 a6 4. Bxc6 dxc6), as explained in Principle 109.

Many opening and middlegame ideas are based on possible subsequent endgame positions. So it is necessary to know those basic endgame positions in order to thoroughly understand the previous opening and middlegame positions.

Endgames are studied the least because any specific endgame position comes up less often than pet opening or middlegame positions, and therefore probably seem less important. But laziness and lack of understanding should never blind you to just how basic endgame positions are to true chess knowledge.

♟ ♞ ♜ ♛

Without thoroughly understanding the basic building blocks of any discipline, you cannot master the discipline. Thus in order to master the piano, one must know the scales, arpeggios, and chord progressions in all keys, while in chess, one must know the basic endgame positions in order to master the intricacies of the rest of the game.

Chapter 39

Study

*"Properly taught, a student can learn more in a few hours
than he would find out in 10 years of untutored
trial and error."*

—Emanuel Lasker

Find out what those who have gone before you have learned, and you build up a good foundation of knowledge. Each past master has devoted countless hours to attempting to understand the royal game. Each has had his or her share of success. So it makes sense to study their games, trying to understand what made each tick.

Principle 184: Devour the games of the masters.
When you really understand their play, you will be a master yourself. If you think you understand master chess and have not earned the master rating, you simply understand less than you think you do.

Chess has been played in its current form for well over 200 years. In that time span, millions of master games have been recorded. They are easily available today in many forms. Databases, books, magazines, Web sites, videos, bulletins, and newspaper columns are in libraries, bookstores, at chess clubs, in software, and on the Internet. The games are complete, partial, with full annotation or light notes, or just the bare score. The main point is that they are easily accessible to anyone interested enough in studying them.

Which games should you study? Whatever appeals to you. If the games came from the hand of a master, you can learn something from them. It is probably best to pick a player you admire particularly, or a player whose style appeals to you. Or you could study the games many different masters played in your favorite openings, or study how they handled your favorite openings.

♟ ♞ ♜ ♛

Don't reinvent the wheel. When a vast amount of good material is before you, use it!

Principle 185: Get a teacher, colleague, or even a computer to check all your analysis and ideas.

You have to check all the analysis and ideas yourself in the end, but don't do it all yourself. Use whatever resources are available to you. Strong computer programs are available, and some of them are even programmed to show you better moves and explain why they are better.

Another great source of chess knowledge is the opponent you just got through struggling with. Whatever the result of the game, this person has stared at the same positions that you have for a long time, and probably has some insights you may have missed. Analyze the game with him or her if you possibly can.

Of course the best way to improve, if not the cheapest, is to get a good instructor. There are many chess masters who also teach, and you can probably find somebody you can work with. If there is no one in your area, Internet instruction, e-mail instruction, or even U.S. Postal service instruction (snail mail) will serve. Failing individual instruction, there are chess camps and chess classes available in some areas. Check into it by getting in touch with the U.S. Chess Federation (3054 US Route 9W, New Windsor, NY 12553, 845-362-8350 ext. 130, *www.uschess.org*, or *scholastic@uschess.org*).

♟ ♞ ♜ ♛

No one is an island. Get the help you need. It is readily available.

Principle 186: One of the best ways to learn is to subject your own games to intensive analysis.

Studying your own games is the other side of the learning process. This is a very important part of your program if you are interested in improving. In fact, I am tempted to call this your most important activity in chess mastery. It is your game you are trying to improve, after all. What better way than to dig into your own play and find out what you are doing right and what you are doing wrong. From there, you build on those things you do right and correct those you do wrong.

The theory is simple enough. Of course, it is not an easy thing to admit you are making mistakes, particularly if they are in a part of your game you may be proud of. You have to approach your own games from a completely objective standpoint, and here is one way in which it is so helpful to have another player, computer, or teacher help you in searching out your errors. This is so hard to do without help from outside. Review Chapter 23 again if it isn't clear why Principle 186 is so important.

♟ ♞ ♜ ♛

Any time you learn something about yourself you are giving yourself a chance to improve. By learning what kind of player you are, you can know yourself so much better. Study anything you do any time you wish to find a way to better yourself.

Principle 187: Study the game notes of top players. Learn the way they think in various positions, and imitate them.

This is simply a specific way to implement principles 184 and 185. By focusing on the thinking process of better layers you learn to imitate it.

Richard Reti once said that he could find any of Alexander Alekhine's great combinations given the same positions, but he couldn't figure out how the great one came up with the positions in the first place. That's the real task—to find out how players you admire and want to emulate think throughout the game. How do they approach the openings? What makes them choose one middlegame structure over another? If a position reminds them of something from the past, what was the key to this recognition?

Studying the thought processes of the masters will give you an insight into what you should be thinking about during a game.

♟ ♞ ♜ ♛

Delve into the thought processes of the great ones if you have any aspirations at all. Imitation is the sincerest form of flattery.

Principle 188: Supplement your study with practice. The combination of the two is indispensable to a true understanding of the game.

If this looks a bit familiar, it's only because you are remembering Principle 179. But this time, you have some study to supplement.

Playing many chess games against different opponents is the only way to make anything you have learned about chess take root. You will not really understand isolated pawn positions, for instance, until you have played a number of them, preferably some where the isolated pawn is yours and some where your opponent is the one who handles it. You will also never learn how to handle an aggressive counterattacker until you have been forced to deal with aggressive counterattacking play in your games.

Remember, in order to critically examine your play in order to improve, there has to be a game to examine. Study alone will not give you this important tool.

♟ ♞ ♜ ♛

Anyone who has ever taken classes and tests in order to qualify for a job and then went on to do that job knows how little the classes and tests have to do with the actual work. Oh, the information gleaned in the first part is no doubt necessary background, but you never know what to expect until you are actually on the job. That's why experience is such a big asset when looking for work.

Chapter 40

Passion

*"(Siegbert) Tarrasch had outplayed me in the opening, but he
lacked the passion that whips the blood when great stakes can
be gained by resolute and self-confident daring."*
—Emanuel Lasker, *American Chess Bulletin*, 1908

If chess has not captured your soul, you probably will not do as well
as one who is enthralled by Caissa. It's simply a matter of how important the game is for you. A casual player will never reach the heights a
dedicated, addicted player can reach. Even if he does, such success
won't mean as much to him.

Principle 189: Thoroughly enjoy the game.
Let's be real: chess is not a serious activity. It is a wonderful game,
but it is a game. If you do not thoroughly enjoy it, you probably
shouldn't be wasting time with it.

I write this knowing full well about the many studies done in
recent years that show how chess improves thinking ability, pattern
recognition, decision making, and a number of other cognitive functions. While this all appears to be true, the tool used to gain all these
wonderful things is still in essence a game that has no inherent use in
and of itself. All these cognitive functions that can be improved
through studying the game are byproducts of the study of chess rather
than the game of chess itself. There are no doubt other ways to
improve cognitive function.

Play chess because you love it. Play it because its intricacies fascinate you. Play it because you love to outthink the other guy. Otherwise, what's the point?

♟ ♞ ♜ ♛

If you are going to spend valuable time on an activity, it is a very good idea to thoroughly enjoy that activity, no matter what wonderful byproducts it can produce. This is the way to make the most of your time, and the most of your life.

Principle 190: When you have an emotional stake in the game, you work harder, remember more, and come up with better ideas. Losses hurt more.

The first part of this principle is one of the main reasons many people don't enjoy competing against computer programs. There is no emotional involvement when an impersonal machine that is programmed to outthink you does so. But when the result makes a difference to you, when winning is important, that's another story.

This is a very hard principle for many people to come to terms with, because when you have an emotional stake in the game, then losing becomes very painful. And you may well have a problem dealing with the pain of losing.

Players have traditionally dealt with the pain of losing in different ways. One is to come up with excuses for losing rather than delving into the actual reasons for losing, which are often correctable. Another is to play weaker players so that losses don't come so often (of course, there will be no improvement in your play when you do it this way). Still another is to crack under the strain whenever a win becomes possible. And yet one more way to deal with the pain of losing is to stop playing. No more games; no more losses. Of course, that last way guarantees no more victories either.

The best way to deal with the pain of losing is to try to learn from each loss so that you do not repeat the same mistakes. Play each position like it is the most important thing in the world to get it right. This

will ultimately give you the best possible results, even though there
will be painful losses along the way.

♟ ♞ ♜ ♛

Emotional involvement puts you at emotional risk, but gives you
the best chance for success. Whenever you love someone or something, the stakes are higher, the potential victory is more satisfying,
and the pain of loss is greater. Accept it, and try your best.

Principle 191: Putting your all into a game will make you a dangerous opponent.

When you are involved in a game and giving it all you have, that's
when you are at your best. You are not afraid of your opponent if he is
rated or ranked higher and do not despise him if he is rated or ranked
lower. Your opponent is just your opponent; someone trying to defeat
you just like you are trying to defeat him. This is what chess is all
about.

In this ideal situation you are not afraid to try a move that looks
right. You will not mind starting a combination if you judge your position to be superior, or defend tenaciously if your position comes under
attack. All you are thinking about is the position at hand and the possibilities that lay ahead.

You are not obsessed with getting a win or holding a draw and are
not terrified of losing. You do not question your analysis during play;
the time to do that is after the game is over. You do not rack up a win
in your mind and stop concentrating on the game or wonder who your
next opponent will be. You do not care which board you are sitting at
or what is going on around you. The game at hand is the thing that has
all your attention!

♟ ♞ ♜ ♛

Any time you put your all into anything, you will be at your best.
Reason enough to always do so, regardless of what it is you are doing.

Chapter 41

Knowledge

There have been more books written about chess than about all other games combined. In addition, there are databases with millions of chess games. You can spend your entire life learning about chess, but you will never learn all there is to know about it or come close to examining every important game that has ever been played.

Principle 192: You cannot know all there is to know about chess.

> *"The game possesses a literature which in contents probably exceeds that of all other games combined."*
> —H. J. R. Murray

Murray wrote this almost one hundred years ago (his *A History of Chess* was first published in 1913). Since then, the literature on chess has expanded exponentially. Obviously, there is no way anyone can process all this information in one lifetime, much less remember it all.

Chess, a subculture all its own, includes many sub-subcultures. Some of these are composed problems, composed endgames, chess variants, correspondence chess, speed chess, chess hustling, chess tournaments, chess politics, various openings, chess set collections, chess camps, chess exhibitions, Internet chess, chess publishing, scholastic chess, and a slew of other chess subcultures too numerous to mention.

For just one example of the plethora of available subcultures, take the openings. There are approximately 500 major opening variations (divided up into five volumes in the *Encyclopedia of Chess Openings*), which include most of the moves and plans that masters have come up with over the last few hundred years. None of the 500 begins with 1. d4 d5 2. e4, which is called the Blackmar-Diemar Gambit. It is not considered a completely sound opening by most masters, and it gets exactly one note in the second edition of Volume D of the *Encyclopedia*.

Yet there are numerous books, collections of games, and Web pages devoted to the Blackmar-Diemar Gambit. The opening is a burning topic in some circles, and when in those circles there's little point in playing anything else.

Obviously, you have to pick and choose what is most important for you if you are going to participate in chess in any way. And choose you will, even if it is to simply read about the game from a safe distance. But if you do decide to plunge in head first, just remember that you can only go so deep. The bottom is untouchable.

♟ ♞ ♜ ♛

A philosopher trying to understand the meaning of life was walking along a beach. He came across his four-year-old son, who was scooping up water from the ocean and pouring it into a sand cup he had constructed. The philosopher was amused and asked his son what he was doing.

"I'm trying to put the ocean in my cup."

"But you can't succeed," his father objected. "The ocean is much too big for your little sand cup."

And the boy replied "Well, the meaning of life is much too big for your brain, yet you don't stop trying to figure it out."

Keep a proper perspective on chess and you won't go wrong.

Principle 193: Understanding is more important than memory.
It's not a good idea to memorize openings until you understand the reasons behind the moves. Otherwise you might play the moves you

know in a slightly different position and get a terrible game. Or you might get it all right but wind up in a position your opponent understands much better than you do. Neither scenario is very good.

For instance, if you don't understand why a healthy pawn majority is better than a doubled pawn complex, there is very little point in playing the Exchange Variation of the Ruy Lopez (1. e4 e5 2. Nf3 Nc6 3. Bb5 a6 4. Bxc6 dxc6). The idea of attempting to exploit this advantage is the whole reason for playing this variation, and White is even willing to part with the bishop-pair in order to do so.

It's even better to play an inferior move that you understand than to copy a move your favorite master played without having a clue as to why the move was played. You have to have some idea of what is going on in the position or you will be hopelessly confused and probably in for a major disappointment.

Never play a move without at least attempting to understand it, and do try to understand every opening variation, combination, or basic endgame you commit to memory.

♟ ♞ ♜ ♛

Understanding is the key to victory. Knowledge is power. Make sure you know what you are doing, and you will always have a better chance at success.

Principle 194: Understanding, supported by memory, is still better than mere understanding.

This is another self-evident principle. The player who understands what she is doing will usually defeat the opponent who has a mass of memorized variations without a clue as to what they mean. But the player who understands what he is doing without a lot of book knowledge to supplement this knowledge will invariably lose to the opponent who also understands what she is doing but has a large background of memorized variations to back up her understanding.

This is why it is so dangerous to go into one of the popular tactical variations such as the Yugoslav Attack in the Dragon Variation of the Sicilian Defense (1. e4 c5 2. Nf3 d6 3. d4 cxd4 4. Nxd4 Nf6 5. Nc3 g6 6. Be3 Bg7 7. f3 0-0 8. Qd2). If you haven't studied many games and side variations and supported your study by playing the variations in many of your own games, you cannot expect to live very long against experts in these variations. Understanding alone will not compete against the tactical finds of so many great players over the years. And much of this knowledge is published all over the place.

So if you are unsure about your opponent, or know her to be an expert at the variation, it is best to play more positional variations, where the tactical complexity isn't so great.

♟ ♞ ♜ ♛

Understanding may beat memorization, but understanding along with memorization will defeat understanding alone. Again, knowledge is power, provided it is real knowledge. But deeper, fuller knowledge backed up with memorization is better yet.

Principle 195: Know the basic endgame positions.

This is the time when the combined understanding and variations of Principle 194 can come in handy. Basic endgame positions are important to know because they show the strength and weakness of each piece and each pawn. Instead of trying to understand thirty-two chess pieces in various configurations, like you attempt to do in the openings, these basic endgames contain nothing more than a king for each side along with a piece or a pawn or two for each side.

Working with three, four, five, or six pieces on an otherwise empty board can be an exacting science. Nevertheless, once you understand what each side is trying to accomplish and how it can be accomplished in various configurations, you will be better equipped to comprehend more complex positions. For this reason, the player who knows the basic endgames cold will be a much better player overall than one who does not know these positions.

First attempt to grasp the fundamentals before trying to move on to more complex knowledge. More complex situations are always combinations of the various fundamentals.

Principle 196: Know the basic tactical themes.

This principle is different from Principle 195 only in specifics. This time we are talking about tactical fundamentals rather than endgame fundamentals, but the idea is very similar. Knowing what each piece can do by itself is essential to understanding what it can do in combination with other pieces and pawns.

When you know the capabilities of each piece separately, then you are ready to combine them in more complex variations. Only when you know each tactical theme separately will you be able to combine them into sizzling combinations.

This same principle applies to strategic, opening, and pawn structure principles as well. The idea is that you must know the fundamentals before you can go on to more complex combinations that bring these various fundamentals together.

♟ ♞ ♜ ♛

You must be able to crawl before you can walk, and walk before you can run. A musician will never be able to move her audience if she is incapable of playing the fundamental scales on her instrument. The complex is a natural extension of the various simple fundamentals. Know them and you are well on your way to real understanding.

Chapter 42

Excuses

Why do you lose? Finding excuses for not performing at your best is easy to do. But it can also retard possible later improvement by taking your attention away from the real problems.

> *"Chess is a matter of vanity."*
> —Alexander Alekhine, *Chess Review*, 1934

> *"Chess contradicts the hypocrite. ... the merciless*
> *combination ends in checkmate."*
> —Emanuel Lasker

Principle 197: Making excuses for losing will not help you win more games.

When was the last time you defeated a completely healthy opponent? So many players make excuses about bad health after losing that you begin to wonder if anybody is ever healthy. You get the impression that if they were, they would trounce you all the time. Hmmm. That may not be the true state of affairs.

When you lose, or at least you don't win, there is a tendency to find excuses for your failure: "I didn't feel so good, I was tired, I was distracted, or other things were on my mind." The problem with these excuses is that they are not productive.

Excuses do not get at the real reason for your failure: Why you made less-than-stellar moves or conceived of inappropriate plans; the reason you didn't understand a key position as well as your opponent did. It may be because you simply don't understand such positions as well as you would like, or you didn't concentrate hard enough on the position because your thinking is not disciplined. Real reasons for failure are quite different from the excuses most people give.

♟ ♞ ♜ ♛

Excuses may salvage your pride for a while, but they will not help you to do better in the future. That's why they can be counterproductive. It's better to look for actual reasons for failure rather than make excuses (Principle 198).

Principle 198: Find the real reason things went wrong, and work to make sure it doesn't happen again.

Chess is supposed to be a game of the intellect. Each player strives to outthink the other. When fatigue and distractions find their way into the game, the players will often not perform at their best. Therefore, if you got distracted or your lack of sleep caught up with you, there is something you can do to prevent this from happening in the future. Namely, discipline your thinking or get more sleep. Any less-than-optimal condition that you put up with will indeed prevent you from doing your best.

When such conditions are inevitable due to no fault of your own, you can still work hard to concentrate on the game at hand. A big part of this is working on your powers of concentration when practicing. That way you will have good concentration habits, and distractions shouldn't have such a large impact on you.

Once your concentration is in full gear, then you can focus on whatever chess-related problems you may have. This is the area you need to study the most in order to improve.

♟ ♞ ♜ ♛

The problem with having good concentration powers is that you then lose most of the usual excuses for failure. Of course, this is also the greatest part of possessing those powers. Without excuses getting in the way, you have a chance to greatly improve your strength and understanding. Isn't that what it's all about?

Principle 199: Learn from your defeats, your draws, and your victories.

Every game should be a learning experience, whether you play it, read about it, or witness it in some other way. Every position you contemplate should be a learning experience.

Failing to learn from the games and positions you are exposed to sentences you to perpetual commission of these errors. These can be understanding, calculation, logical thinking, or concentration errors. Forgetting what you have done will not help you to improve in any way.

Learning from losses is obvious, especially if your opponent was stronger than you and outplayed you. But what if your opponent was weak and you were simply careless? That should also be obvious: Learn not to take opponents so lightly in the future, and learn to be careful in all situations. For example, if you fell for a simple trap, then learn to watch out for such traps in the future.

You can also learn from draws, whether of the well-played variety or the mistake-filled variety. In the former case, you can submit the game to intensive analysis and try to find where either player missed opportunities to improve. In the latter case, identify the mistakes and try to make sure they do not happen again. One type of draw it's hard to learn from is the nongame. If you and your opponent play a couple of moves and shake hands, then you never really played chess at all.

Learning from your wins is similar to learning from your losses and draws in that you probably did not play perfect chess. You can examine the game with a magnifying glass to find out where you—or your opponent—could have improved. This is similar to learning from the games of the masters except that it has more of an emotional impact on you.

Regardless of the end result, anything you do can be a learning experience in life. It's a matter of being in the right frame of mind. If you want to learn anything at all or to improve any aspect of your life, simply pay attention to what you do and analyze it afterwards. Then go out and do it again, only better.

Principle 200: You will get out of chess what you put into it.

This is probably the most obvious of all the principles. Yet so many people feel that they are unlucky or that the deck is stacked against them. Some feel that they can never improve no matter what. This may be how a person thinks who is in the midst of a losing streak.

But losing streaks are temporary. They are indeed a part of the game, and you will suffer them if you play regularly. This is, of course, no big deal if you have the attitude that you can learn from your losses. But it becomes very hard to convince yourself you are learning as the losses pile up.

Of course, winning and losing are only part of the game. A big part, perhaps, but only part. The beauty of a well-calculated combination or a hidden strategic idea is also part of chess, as is the excitement we feel whenever we see or execute a powerful sacrifice, or even a potentially powerful sacrifice. The exhilaration of competition and the joy of coming up with clever ideas are also part of the game. So are the people that get involved. Chess is a social activity, and getting to know the people in the chess world and interacting with them is a very important part of the overall experience.

However deeply you may become involved with chess, however strong a player you may become, the rewards will be in direct proportion to the effort you have put into it.

♙ ♘ ♖ ♛

This is something we all know intuitively. In the long run, our enjoyment of something is in direct proportion to the efforts we make to achieve it. That is the way of life. That is Tao.

About the Author

Peter Kurzdorfer is the former editor of *Chess Life* magazine and the author, along with the U.S. Chess Federation, of *The Everything®Chess Basics Book*. Mr. Kurzdorfer has been a Chess Master since the early 1980s, earning his Master rating in 1981 and the Original Life Master title in 1991. He began teaching chess in the 1980s and served as Resident Chess Master in Bradford, PA, throughout most of the 1990s. He lives in Franklinville, NY.